"Own what you know."

Nancy D. Solomn

Praise for

Impact!

"Nancy Solomon's treasure of a book is punctuated with real examples you can use to create a life on *your own terms*. Nancy delivers inspiration from the heart combined with common sense for everyday living. I thoroughly enjoyed her down-to-earth approach, coupled with her delightful sense of humor. This is a treat you won't want to miss."
—**Chérie Carter-Scott**, Ph.D., author of *If Life Is a Game, These Are the Rules: Ten Rules for Being Human*

"Do yourself a favor: Buy, read, think about, and implement *Impact!* Nancy Solomon is a front-runner who inspires you to solve problems, navigate life's challenges and victories, and set a powerful direction for your life. While inspiring, humorous, and candid, *Impact!* is a serious book that directly challenges the beliefs women hold about themselves—the same beliefs that hold them back. If you're ready to lead from within, you're ready for *Impact!*"
—**Sarah Weddington**, winning attorney, *Roe v. Wade*; professor, University of Texas at Austin

"Nancy Solomon has written a book that is both loving and empowering. It's an inspirational and practical gem for women—and men—at all phases of career and life."
—**Rick Foster**, co-author of *How We Choose to Be Happy* and *Choosing Brilliant Health*

"When women decide to move out of the shadows from invisibility and to own their invincibility, remarkable things happen. Thanks to Nancy Solomon for inspiring women to champion their unique light and share it with the sisterhood and the entire world. It's a great way for women to live in the flow of life where expansive things can happen."
—**Yitta Halberstam**, author of *Small Miracles*

"Author Nancy Solomon asks you to 'consider how much grit it takes to put your life in full view of everyone you care about and respect.' Her book, *Impact!*, is a heapin' helpin' of grit, served up with a side order of 'you had it in you all along.'"
—**Maureen Anderson**, host of *The Career Clinic*® radio program

Impact!

Impact!

What Every Woman Needs to Know to Go From Invisible to Invincible

NANCY D. SOLOMON

John Wiley & Sons, Inc.

Published by John Wiley & Sons, Inc., Hoboken, New Jersey.
Published simultaneously in Canada.

For general information on our other products and services or for technical support, please contact our Customer Care Department within the United States at (800) 762-2974, outside the United States at (317) 572-3993 or fax (317) 572-4002.

Wiley also publishes its books in a variety of electronic formats. Some content that appears in print may not be available in electronic books. For more information about Wiley products, visit our web site at www.wiley.com.

ISBN 978-0-470-48439-5

Printed in the United States of America.

10 9 8 7 6 5 4 3 2 1

To my beloved brother, Bruce,
who taught me everything there is to know about love;
and to my daughter, Lily, and my son, Benjamin,
who remind me every day.

Contents

Acknowledgments

When I was 11 years old I declared that, one day, I would write a book. That dream has just been fulfilled. Between then and now I have had more blessings than could possibly be recorded on these pages, or on a hundred like them. I have known countless people who have allowed me the privilege of loving them. I have taught thousands of men and women who thought I was the teacher when, in truth, I was the student. For every single one of you who have touched my heart and entered my life, and for those who will, one day, I am more grateful than could ever be expressed.

This book is a tribute to the hearts and minds of women, so, naturally, I want to celebrate the first and most influential woman in my life, my mother, Gloria Solomon. It is an absolute joy to be your daughter. I honor you and your choices, I know your strength, and I admire the courage it took to lead our family. Every day I silently thank you for those tea parties and for insisting that I learn how to type.

To Bernard Solomon, with you as my father I learned how to stand in my power with dignity and grace. I am eternally grateful.

To Lily Joy, who shares my soul, and Benjamin Bruce, who owns my heart—I love you more than every grain of sand on every beach. Thank you for the privilege of parenting you, and for the stretch marks that you leave on my heart.

There is no way to adequately express the love and respect I have for my much younger sister, Ami Kaplan, who is chairwoman of my fan club. The love in your heart and the generosity of your spirit is always with me. You will never know the depth of my gratitude for your unwavering support, and your chicken potpie crust. Howard— thank you for your patient listening and calm voice. Lindsay, Wesley, and Madison—may you continue to love like there's no tomorrow, and may you remember to give back in excess of what you've been given. Each of you has your own place in my heart.

A special tribute to my Grammy, who taught me what it means to be invincible, and my fairy godmother, Marian Snitkoff, who always reminded me to take my "yougly pills"—I can only hope that the impact I leave is as loving and unselfish as that which both of you left me.

To Helene Gardner, my aunt, for introducing me to elegance, style, and Europe—merci beaucoup! Bill Gardner—you put the fun back in family—I love you!

To one of the finest human beings I have ever been blessed to know—Chuck Shelton. God must have been having a particularly great day when he introduced us. You have changed my world, opened my eyes, revealed my heart, and shared my calamari. You remind me of who I am whenever I forget, and for that God thanks you! To Suzanne, Melinda, and Patrick—thanks for adopting the Solomons into your hearts and for sharing so many special moments with us.

To my dearest friend, Irene Turner, who has traveled many long and winding roads with me and has never once let me get lost for very long. Your belief in me and my gifts, your absolute trust and faith in who I am and what I bring to the world, and your willingness to give it to me straight and compassionately is one of my life's greatest blessings. If my friends are my wealth, you have made me a gazillionaire.

Every woman needs a Curt Rosengren—from the beginning you have been honest, direct, supportive, my fan and, when necessary, your foot has been on my tush—thank you for letting me count on you and for never once having let me down. Chuck Pettet, your influence is why this book is here today—much gratitude for the generosity with which you share yourself. Shawn Frodsham, for the past 14 years you have been an unwavering force in my life. You are precious to me and I will always cherish our late night tune-ins.

Every working mom needs a nanny with a laptop—we have our Dexter Reuhl. Your life purpose is "support" and you are a master at it! Sometimes God's angel committee works overtime and that was the case when Rabbi Zalman and Miriam Heber entered our lives—thank you for bringing me home. Baruch Hashem!

When it was time for a reality check, I counted on my review committee Aggie, Alicia, Amy, Chuck, Kim, Lisa, Paige, Pauline, and

Valerie—you did a remarkable job making sure that every word was in service to *Impact*'s readers. In gratitude!

Yvonne Oswald—newest member of my angel committee—you are as great as your word.

I am blessed to have met David Brake and Holly McAllister of Authorbound/Content Connections—there is no doubt in my mind that this book would never have been born had you not taken me under your wings, guided me firmly and lovingly, and given me a wake-up call when I was in need of one. Your expertise, wisdom, and complete faith in me allowed me to give myself permission to write *Impact!* I am indebted to you both.

The juiciest thanks go to every one of you who have allowed me the privilege to do what I love to do most. I've adored working with you!

In memory of Ross Anderson, who saw me way before I did, and Susan L. Shulman, whose life was her purpose.

Message from the Author
Just between You and Me

Over the course of many incarnations in the personal growth field, I have had the incomparable honor of standing before thousands of women from all over the world. In a multitude of roles I have spoken on behalf of myself, in defense of others, and on the part of women who, however incorrectly, perceived that I have a voice greater than their own. The truth is that my unabashed passion, my brazen enthusiasm, and my lack of personal censure about women and their power has taken me by surprise far more than it has anybody else. Sometimes, when I reflect on the bodaciousness of my mission, it embarrasses me. Most of the time, though, it merely makes me giggle.

The privilege of speaking to and for women is both a blessing and a test; while the former is rather clear, the latter requires a bit of explanation. There is an awesome responsibility that comes with having a mouth as big as my heart. The test comes from having the courage to stay true to myself, to keep my message pure and in integrity, and to not sway because someone won't like me, or they may think I'm not intelligent, or not enough of one thing and too much of another.

I believe that, over the course of the past 20 years, I have succeeded in conveying the message that threads women, courage, and impact together in the same breath with far more success than failure in those same efforts. Not incidentally, it is the failures that persist in staying with me the longest, and it is in that which I commune with all women. (However unfortunate, we women have a predisposition to martyr ourselves with our failures, rather than elevate ourselves with our accomplishments.)

At this point in my life, few stories still carry enough adrenaline to lift my eyebrows too far out of place. I am, nonetheless, still surprised by the ease with which women willingly relate their life stories, with the eagerness they demonstrate in doing so, and with the lack of pretense with which this takes place.

I have spent many hours listening to the shocking tales—the ones that depict the travesties that are committed against women, between women, and, most sadly, on women by themselves.

I have stood in the holy space of some of the rawest questions, ones that will likely never be partnered with answers. "How could this have happened to me?" "What did I do to deserve this?" "How do I learn to love myself?" Too many times I have been silenced by the shame they have carried.

I have cried with many of these women as I gripped them to my chest, their snot and tears dripping down the front of both of us, while they downloaded the emotional wreckage of their lives. I have bitten my tongue so that I wouldn't gasp at some atrocity a woman was sharing. More than once, I have cried myself to sleep over the misery of another woman's life.

Curiously, the stories I've been privy to strengthen my resolve to assist and support women. Never once have I ever wanted to retreat from the job I consider to be my own: the job of listening and tending to the wounded heart and rejuvenating the aching spirit, of mining the treasures, of celebrating the victories, of turning lower case push back into upper case ACCOMPLISHMENT. Never once have I been too disillusioned to continue, too angry to be quiet, or too frightened not to care.

Although not in equal measure, I have also guffawed with women until the tears of laughter streaked my face, the warm liquid pooling at the neck of my stained shirt. I have giggled uncontrollably and shrieked with delight at both the foibles and fantasies that women will share, given a safe and caring place to do so. Some of us girls can bend toward vulgarity and shock, both intentionally and not, given the right atmosphere and the perfect audience. I'll admit, right here, that I have participated equally in both.

I have clung to my aching ribs when I couldn't quite catch my breath between laughing fits. I have succumbed more often than I should have to breaching professional boundaries when comparing and sharing my own truth seemed the only genuine thing to do. I have never regretted doing so.

We women love to share and we love to commiserate: We bond over trouble, over love, over food, and over sex. We seal these connections with hope, with prayers, with tears, and with chocolate. These things make many of us, most of the time, very content, if not darn happy.

I can honestly report that I have never met one single woman without a dream, a hope, a vision, or a prayer. I have never met one woman who, in private, denied having an intuition, one who didn't seek permission to be who she already is, or one who had never chosen failure over regret.

I have never met a woman who didn't, at least once, apologize for being outstanding, one who didn't ache to fit in and belong, or one who wasn't willing to self-deprecate in order to comfort a crowd. I have never met a woman who didn't censure her own achievements, nor have I met one who didn't, on occasion, pretend to be a refrigerator bulb when she was, in truth, a stadium light. Most women I have met have gone several rounds with all the above.

During all my travels, I have never met a woman who had never questioned whether she was an imposter, or one who hadn't compared herself to Mother Teresa or Gloria Steinem or Pamela Anderson. Of course, it was not in that order.

I have never met a woman who didn't argue for, while simultaneously resent, her own limitations, nor have I ever met a woman who failed to compare her accomplishments with others'. I have never encountered a woman who consistently focused on her strengths, one who felt no competitiveness with her sister, or one who wished for her bottom to be bigger than it was. I have never met a woman whose inner girlfriend had truly ever deserted her, and I have never known a grown woman who didn't have a secret.

I have seldom met a woman who, when knocked down by the drift of the culture, wasn't perfectly capable of picking herself up and carrying on with dignity. I have seldom met a woman who easily surrendered her fight for self-esteem, or one who couldn't muster up a bit of grace when she truly needed to. Nor have I met more than a woman or two who didn't secretly covet something, anything, trimmed in marabou.

The women I have known best have been starved for attention, anxious for love, and desperate for the truth. They may have read all the self-improvement books, listened to all the motivational CDs, attended all the requisite seminars, and, at the end of the day, really just wanted someone to love them exactly and precisely as they were in that moment (especially if they were having a fat day).

Above all else, the women I have met have served most purposefully to reinforce my truest sense of what is right and just and beautiful in our world. They have been strong and proud and fierce in their determination to show up in their own lives, and make a difference in the lives of their families and in the heartbeat of their community.

This book is focused on everything that is right about being a woman—our gifts, our talents, our strengths, our intellect, our humor, our softness, our edges, our truth, and even the lies we tell about ourselves when we are pretending we aren't as amazing as we truly are.

This book is dedicated to those women I have met, to the ones I have yet to meet, and to the ones I may never personally meet, but with whom I will always connect in spirit and, if only, by gender. This book is dedicated to the essence of the feminine, the strength of our anatomy, and the power we house in our hearts.

Consider *Impact!* the longest thank-you note ever written. It was created for all the women about whom I have just written, in thanks for their allowing me to support them. I appreciate you more than you will ever know.

This book is also written for all the women who have, in turn, supported me. It is for those of you who, knowingly or not, have had any size impact on my life and on my soul, and who may have said any one thing that has made a difference. For some it was your presence alone that altered my perception of what it is to be a woman, and what it is to be me.

This is my very best attempt to acknowledge the contribution that you are—even knowing, as I say this, that it is impossible to fully do so. I hope my words—my ideas, thoughts, and experiences—shed light on who you are, on what you do, and on how and why you impact the world.

Reader Self-Assessment

What has been proven over and over again is that written goals are many times more likely to be reached than those that we merely 'think about' in our heads. With that in mind, I invite you to get clear and specific about why you chose this book, and what you will change in your life once you've read it. How do you want this book to impact your life? How will it impact the other people in your life once you've read it? Have fun with this!

Place a check next to the phrases that best describe what you plan to accomplish by reading *Impact!*

- ☐ Open up to new relationships
- ☐ Learn to put myself first instead of last
- ☐ Have more power to speak up for myself
- ☐ Feel like I'm in charge instead of out of control
- ☐ More balance in my life
- ☐ Know my purpose and be on purpose
- ☐ Know that I add value and communicate that to others
- ☐ Know that I deserve more than this
- ☐ Know that I'm worthy of love and respect
- ☐ Get to know myself better
- ☐ Believe in myself so I don't have so many doubts
- ☐ Step out of my comfort zone and take more risks
- ☐ Have more of a connection to myself and others
- ☐ Allow myself to make mistakes without guilt or shame
- ☐ Have more confidence
- ☐ Be less stressed
- ☐ Refuel and have more energy
- ☐ Feel lighter
- ☐ Have a plan for one year and five years
- ☐ Figure out what I want and act on it

☐ Courage to pursue my dreams
☐ Increase my ability to positively impact others.
☐ Leave a lasting, meaningful legacy
☐ Get people to listen to me
☐ Get respect for my point of view
☐ Stand up to bullies and aggressive people
☐ Learn how to be a better leader
☐ Discover how to say what I mean
☐ Be more assertive
☐ Learn how to get recognition
☐ Be more appreciated
☐ Bring all of me to work
☐ _____
☐ _____
☐ _____
☐ _____
☐ _____

Introduction
One More Load of Laundry before I Die

"Whoa! Wait just one New York minute!" I thought. "I can't die. I haven't gotten *it* done yet." I panicked. I was sweating and pleading. I groveled, "God please give me one more chance to finish; I'll get *it* right. I promise."

My hysteria escalated not because I was ill, not because I was young and vital, and not because I had yet to have children. My alarm went off because I knew, down to my bone marrow, that *it* simply *had* to get done; yet I didn't know what *it* was. All I knew was that I had run out of time.

If you've ever had one of those nightmares where you're running and running—and no matter how fast you run, you don't get anywhere—then you'll have a good sense about my experience. Not only did I not know where I was running, I didn't even know *why* I was running. Except this wasn't a nightmare—it was my life.

It was the fall of 1994, and I had volunteered for a nonprofit whose mission it was to support the families of people living with AIDS. All volunteers were required to receive training in both AIDS Awareness, and Death and Dying. Halfway through the mandatory weekend training, the 20 or so of us had gathered together for a visualization exercise. We were asked to imagine that we were about to die from AIDS, and it was the last few moments of our lives. Lying flat on our backs, eyes closed, we listened to the soothing voice of our instructor as she led us to our death. What were we feeling? What were we thinking? Who was with us? How old were we?

When the ritual was complete and we were all "dead," my classmates and I huddled together to discuss our insights and discoveries. What *were* our last few minutes like? What *did* we think?

"I wanted to know I had made a difference."

"I wanted someone, anyone, to notice I'd gone missing."

"I wanted to leave something of myself behind."

"I wanted to know that my life had counted."

"I wanted more time."

"I'm not finished yet—I have more to do."

_____

_____

Predictably, each one of us had our own unique emotional and mental response to having learned that we would imminently die.

What surprised us, however, was that _every_ single one of us had a distinct, yet vague sense that we'd missed something significant, even urgent, during our lifetime, like missing the main point of our own movie.

In fact, until we did that exercise, none of us had considered that there might even _be_ a point. Yet like a bad dream, each of us had reacted to something we'd sensed had once been there, but was no longer. A shadow of something intangible lingered, leaving us nothing solid to grasp onto or to articulate.

Most of the group was certain that they'd postponed whatever _it_ was for so long that now it would never get done. The mere thought of this missed opportunity tugged at the souls of my new best friends. Like me, they had no idea what _it_ was or why lacking that information so troubled them; they just knew that it did.

While the details of our lives (and imagined deaths) were intensely personal to each one of us, regret was the plasma that ran through us all. The regrets spoken about that day, whether small or insurmountable, seemed to us to be more unbearable than the physical pain we would potentially have felt had we actually been dying of AIDS. It was those regrets—not the deaths of our physical bodies—that we collectively mourned.

During our debriefing, not one person mentioned regretting the relationships they'd had. Neither did anyone wish that they'd had more money, more toys, or more things. None of us voiced despair that we'd not traveled more, or partied less, or done one more load of laundry.

What *did* we talk about? Every single one of us spoke of, and was concerned with, whether we'd made a personally meaningful difference in the world.

We were, decidedly, obsessed with the things we wouldn't get to do in our lives. We were perplexed that we could experience regret for something we wouldn't do in our future, as though we'd arrived in our life scheduled to complete a job that we would now not get to finish. It was the loss of prospective opportunities that saddened us. Listening to my new friends I concluded that there were few hearts that had never been etched with some depth of regret. People are, in some manner, preprogrammed for both concrete and intangible outcomes that, when unfulfilled, incomplete, or unrealized, result in remorse.

The regrets that are linked to our demise fall into one or more of these criteria:

- Some potential hadn't been actualized.
- Some promise had failed to be kept.
- Some plan hadn't been executed.
- Some internal seed had neglected to bloom.

What we wanted most was to have had an *impact*. We decided that this, alone, was the measure by which we could determine whether our lives had been worth living, or whether we'd just taken up space. We identified our impact as the *it* we'd obsessed about in the exercise.

We asked ourselves:

- Had we had an impact?
- What was the impact we'd had?
- Was the drive for impact unique to us, or did others crave the same?

- What creates impact?
- What hinders or deters impact?
- Why was our impact so important to us?
- _____
- _____
- _____

We left at the end of that exhausting day with far more questions than we'd arrived with. All of us committed to contemplating the deeper issues so that when it was, indeed, our time to pass, we would depart with a great sense of achievement.

Since that fall day in 1994, I've spent time with thousands of men and women across the United States. Regardless of whether they were entry-level employees or C-Suite executives, small business owners, professional working moms or stay-at-home dads, retirees or the independently wealthy—the questions that arose that day were never more than an arm's length away. Those conversations, interactions, and relationships became the laboratory in which I explored people's ideas, attitudes, and concerns about the impact they've had in their lives and in the world around them.

What have I learned so far? In my life I had rather fancied myself to be special or unique; on occasion, even extraordinary. And while that may be true in some parts of my life, I discovered that when it comes to the impulse for impact—not so much. Just about everyone I meet and everyone they meet has a deep wired—although often unconscious— urgency to impact their world. And that makes us _all_ special.

In helping thousands of people to discover the source of their impact, their life purpose and all the gifts and talents that support their journey, I have discovered the source of mine. Over the years, I have come to understand and embrace the promise of _my_ life, _my_ purpose, _my_ source of fulfillment. Experimenting with, and living in, these truths and this wisdom gives me license to share them with you.

Each of us is the primary star in our own galaxy. Every one of us has the ability to have a profound and sustainable positive impact on the world. Each one of us has a life purpose that brings peace, clarity, joy, love, and productivity with it; and each of us is at choice as to whether or not we discover it.

The work on these pages is what I have come to do. This is the *it* which so imbalanced me, so shook my core; and made my impending though imaginary death unthinkable. I came to get it done. Now that I know what it is, I can actually do that.

> That's what this book is about: To give you the support, encouragement, skills, tools, and wisdom you'll need to figure out *"why you do what you do."*

By the end of our time together you will know, with absolute certainty:

- ◆ What you came to do
- ◆ Why you came to do it
- ◆ How to get it done
- ◆ How your world impacts you
- ◆ How you can have the most impact in your world
- ◆ Everything you need to know to help you to be the happiest and most successful person you can possibly be

How relevant is this book to *your* life? How can you be sure this is a valuable use of your time?

FACT: You don't have the time *not* to read this book.

Why? Because it's timely, topical, current, and necessary. This book is not a frivolous luxury; it is imperative for those who are committed to making the most of their lives. If you think I'm being dramatic, then consider this:

> The kind of failing economy we're in dictates that your expendability—right *now* in this moment—is directly tied to the impact that you're having on your organization and, ultimately, on your customer.

Out in the real world, where productivity and profit steer the ship, the people who are happiest, most content, most successful and productive are those who are making an impact. They know why they're here, they're aware of their life purpose, and they're making a personally meaningful difference in their own lives and the lives of those around them.

Now, you may be thinking:

- "The economy is in a shambles: I'm so worried about losing my job next month that I just don't have time for this feel-good stuff."
- "I understand that this is important, but I'm just too busy right now."
- "I don't have time; I have to figure out how to recover my recent market losses."
- "When my debt's paid off, I'll think about it."

All this may seem true in a stressful moment; but if you were to take the 10,000-foot view, you'd see that the people who are keeping their jobs, getting recruited, receiving promotions, and earning large bonuses are fewer in number, but more distinguishable than a year ago. They are the ones whose presence and performance has such a high positive impact on their organization that they have become almost indispensible. Is that you?

Take this a step further.

> Corporations are hemorrhaging money right now in direct proportion to the impact—either positive or negative—that they are having on *their* customers, and whether or not those customers are choosing to continue to buy their product or service.

One of this book's most pivotal messages is this: Your impact is one of the only things that you are totally and completely in control of. The person who is ultimately in charge of your life and its impact is sitting in your seat right now (that would be you). The promotion that you didn't get reflects your impact; the raise you *did* receive reflects your impact. The reputation you've earned reflects your impact. You get the idea.

We are busier than ever. Every day, it seems that we have more to do and less time in which to do it. Most of us do not need one more checkable item on our perpetual to-do list: It's become too easy to become overloaded, overworked, and overwhelmed. I wrote this book with all this in mind. In order to accommodate your hectic lifestyle—and in an attempt to reduce your stress—I've deliberately written this book so that most of the essays are three to ten pages long—easy-to-digest portions that you'll find more uplifting than time-consuming. That way, you can read it from cover to cover or randomly.

If you have a 10-minute opening in your schedule, you can jump right in and read any brief section that calls to you. Maybe you'll sift through a few pages while you're waiting for an appointment. A flight is one of the few uninterruptable times in our lives that may be perfect for exploring an exercise or two. Or perhaps you'd prefer to plan some "you" time and click through to my web site (www.frominvisibletoinvincible.com) for assessments, exercises, ideas, and articles. We'd love to have you join our online community, too! Sign up for our daily Solomonisms (aka Windows of Wisdom-WOW), our newsletter or blog. I'll see you there!

I've found it both fun and rewarding to wake up in the morning, take a deep breath, and ask myself what I most need to read or know that day. With my eyes closed, I'll randomly open this book and amazingly discover that the essay I've selected is exactly what I needed to keep me centered and on track all day long. Have a go at it—you'll be surprised and delighted at the result!

What matters most is not how you read this book, but that you *do* read it. I have collected much evidence that our unconscious minds work in partnership with the energy of the universe to supply us with infinite opportunities to live and learn, and to love and grow. Personally, I don't believe in accidents or coincidences. I am, therefore, of the belief that since this book found its way into your hands—that's exactly where it belongs. Congratulations! Your life is about to become a whole lot better than it already is.

Enjoy the journey. I'm with you every step of the way.

Initiate Impact!

1. If you could describe the impact you've made so far in your life, what would you say?
2. How would your coworkers and/or supervisors describe the impact you make on your organization?
3. How would your customers describe this impact?
4. What would you love them to say?

Part One

What Is Impact?

Essay 1

Impact Is the Fingerprint,
Not the Finger That Printed It
All You Leave Is Your Impact

"All you leave is your impact." That thought lifted me out of a pool of tears one afternoon as I left the hospital, having just said good-bye to my dear client, Elaine Childs-Gowell. Elaine had suffered a massive stroke, and I knew it would be the very last time I'd see her alive (if you could call a coma alive).

Had it been anyone else, I might have used the words "final farewell"; but there was nothing final about anything Elaine had ever done. Her loving-kindness, empathic spirit, good sense, and unending wisdom will stay with me until the moment I am the one lying in a bed somewhere—with any of my unused potential in a puddle around me.

Elaine was a psychiatric nurse practitioner who had written several books and traveled the world teaching (healing and shamanism); she had a slew of initials trailing her name. Watching this dear woman lying there with her life force replaced by a morphine drip, I realized that more than the books and articles she wrote or the classes and speeches she gave, what she'd really leave behind was her passion for people and the impact that had. That was all; and it was plenty.

> When our own time comes, few people will remember what we did, or even how we did it. What *will* stay with others is how they felt when they were with us, and maybe what they felt when they thought about us.

The indelible print is how someone made us feel about ourselves; what emotional taste that relationship left in our mouths. Time erodes the details that caused the dread or delirium that we experienced. All details fade into the background, and what is left is the impact of that moment—and how it carries forth to this day.

"Think of impact as the fingerprint, not as the finger that printed it."

- ◆ Your impact is not what you did, but the consequence of this action.
- ◆ Your impact is not what you said, but the outcome that came from your saying it.
- ◆ Your impact is not what you thought, but the action that sprang from your ideas.

> When we impact people, we become the catalyst that helps them to activate their latent life purpose.

Some spark within people is ignited—just by virtue of having connected with us—that reminds them of their personal DNA for greatness. Our impact triggers the memory that they came here to get something done; that they, too, made a promise, and the note has come due.

■ ■ ■

I don't recall precisely what Mrs. Claire Tornay taught me in fourth grade, but I do remember the magnitude of her belief in me. She was the first person ever to tell me that I was *really* smart, and that I could do anything I set my mind to. I acted on her faith in me as though it was the absolute Truth, with a capital T; which, of course, made it so. When I was in her presence, I stood a little taller, was a tad more confident, and I eagerly focused my attention on the things I did well. I can't be sure that any of this is factually true; but I can tell you that my memory of it is that she thought I was destined for great things, that I was worthy and lovable, and that I was smart in my head *and* my heart. Doors still open today because of those feelings that Mrs. Tornay stirred.

Ditto for my chemistry professor, Mr. Dennis Clancy. I was in lab with my regular class the day my mind enviously wandered off to the gorgeous twins at the next table. They were size zeroes, popular with the 'in' crowd, and wore the ID bracelets of the school hunks. Thinking I was alone in my reverie, I longingly stared at them as I wondered what it would be like to be a foot shorter and a single digit size. By then I had already reached my full height of five feet eleven inches, and I was born bigger than the twins were in high school. (I might be exaggerating.)

Mr. Clancy caught my eye and, out of the blue, said, "You have a classic beauty that will never grow old." He left me standing there baffled by his comment. It was probably 20 years before I realized that he had read my thoughts that day, and the beauty he spoke of had to do with my soul—not my size. There were many dark days when I retrieved his comment from the back rooms of my spirit and held them as a life preserver, to keep me from drowning in the sorrow and disappointment that escorted depression through the first half of my life.

You see, it wasn't what either Mrs. Tornay or Mr. Clancy actually *did* that made one shred of difference in my life. It was neither their comments nor their deeds that influenced me to transcend my doubts and transform my potential into something worth leaving behind. It was how they *held* me that made every difference then, and continues to do the same thing to this day. Both of them perceived me as a winner, when I clung to the cloak of loser. They *held* me as worthy, when I couldn't see a trace of value. They *held* me as a treasure, when I felt like crap. They *held* me as no one had done before. That was their impact.

■ ■ ■

You have undoubtedly had people do the same for you—whether you're aware of it or not. For some it was your parents, grandparents, or siblings. For others, it was a neighbor, a friend, a grocer, a stranger. Most of these acts were not deliberate; they were subtle accidents of nature committed by people who, in all likeliness, were not conscious of what they were doing—and were ignorant of the impression they'd left.

You've surely thought about these people. Every once in a while, they appear in your mind; you wonder what made you remember them at that moment. Thinking of them brings a smile, a twinge, a smirk, a tear. Is it time for you to tell someone about the impact they had in your life, in your heart, on your success?

Quickly—before you have a moment to censor yourself—ask out loud, "Who has most impacted my life?" (No editing: If you sense it was the Queen of England, write it down. Likewise, if it was the school janitor, or a relative or friend whose name has long been forgotten—write it down.) Right below this person's name, jot a few words to describe the impact that he or she has had on your life.

1. Name_____
Impact_____
2. Name_____
Impact_____
3. Name_____
Impact_____
4. Name_____
Impact_____
5. Name_____
Impact_____

What you don't know, what you might never know, is who you yourself impacted.

That lighthearted remark, that unsolicited hand you lent, that word of encouragement or phrase of feedback, that timely wink or lapse of memory—all of it, unquestionably, has left its mark. The only question is what kind of mark it left. Did it encourage or discourage its recipient? Did it pick someone up or—quite unintentionally—put someone down? Did it raise the stakes or lower the bar? Did that person feel heinous or heroic, lovable or laughable, powerful or pitiful?

Although it is impossible to predetermine precisely how any individual will react to you or your actions, there are some things in the impact department that are well within your accountability range.

- ◆ *Know your intention.* It is the intentions behind your actions, rather than the actions themselves, that are most significant. Your intentions will linger long after you are gone.
- ◆ *Live your life purpose.* Anything you do that is in accordance with that which you came here to do will be passionate, positive, productive, and practical.
- ◆ *Demonstrate right use of will.* What separates you from lower life forms is your ability to reason and make choices. So make good ones.
- ◆ *Err on the side of love.* Always. Love yourself first, and all else will harmoniously flow. While you may come to the end of your life with a few regrets, the way you treated others will not be one of them.

■ ■ ■

I learned some of these rules from someone I met through business and who has, over the course of a few decades, become my best friend and colleague. Chuck Shelton is one of a handful of elite members of the Highly Functional Family Society; he is also the first and only member of that club whom I have ever personally met. Chuck and his family are the poster people for healthy, loving, and nurturing families. While I did indeed ask them to adopt me, I was told that they do not have honorary family memberships; and I am too old to be adopted anyway. Oh, well, it was worth asking, right?

I could go on at length about Chuck's career success in leadership development; about the profound influence his book has had on
diversity in this country; or about the extraordinary commitment he
has to God. All that, however, would be eclipsed by the emotional
and spiritual impact he has on everyone who knows him or who has
experienced him vicariously through his work.

Over the years, I have spent some time with Chuck's parents as well
as with his wife and two children. Witnessing the relationship between
all three generations has been a miracle in my life. I recall the time when
his daughter Melinda was playing basketball in high school with a coach
who was, on occasion, demotivating, unfair, and to say the least, not
supportive. Melinda, a leader in her own right, had just about had it
with his attitude. She decided that no matter what, she would resist the
coach's domination. Her family stood by, supported, encouraged, and
defended her. It's easy to see that the genuine love between them is
the glue that keeps them strong and powerful as individuals, as well as
a family unit.

I asked Chuck about his parents' impact on him. He told me this
story: When he was 11 years old, he defended an unpopular boy and
was verbally humiliated in front of the class, at length, by a teacher. He
stood his ground, and told his mother about it when he returned home.
The next day, Mary Shelton confronted the principal and the teacher;
the teacher was transferred out of elementary education the following year.

I asked Chuck what he gained from that experience and what he
had learned from being parented by Mary and Beck. Here's what he
told me:

- He could stand up for what was right even against adults, even
  though he was young.
- He could share his hurt with his mom.
- His mom would use her power to stand up for him.
- He would have power to use on behalf of his own kids.

Once he had finished sharing the story, I made some comment
about the apple not falling far from the tree. He asked me what I

meant. I'd observed that Chuck's lessons that day were identical to the ones Melinda learned in confronting her coach's behavior. We know that past behavior is a predictor of future behavior; so now all of us know what the impact of the Sheltons will be on the next generation, and on the generations after that.

When I became a parent myself, I looked to the Sheltons as role models for ideal parenting. I was determined to raise my family with the same consciousness and values I'd learned from them. Chuck had learned about the responsibility that comes with having impact very early in his life; one can only imagine where his parents had learned the same values.

■ ■ ■

While you may never know what your impact has been, it is guaranteed that you have had one. You are not in charge of how anyone will receive you into their lives—no matter how long or fleeting your moment of interface.

> You are not in charge of whether the receptor dials of others are tuned to love or to fear; and you cannot will them to embrace the gift that you are, or the gifts that you bring.

The only thing that you will know for sure on the day you pass from this life is whether you made your life count—because deep in your soul, you'll know that all you'll be leaving is your impact. You are responsible for the impact you have on others, and for the way you manage the impact they have on you.

Initiate Impact!

1. What do you notice about the people who have had the most impact on your life?
   - Do they have anything in common with one another?

- What role have they played in your life?
- How have they had impact on your personal life or your professional life—or both?

2. How do you impact the people in your life?
   - How will they remember you?
   - How is this different from how you want them to remember you?
   - What role have you played in their lives?
   - How will your "leave-behind" be spiritual, emotional, mental, and/or physical?

3. How does the organization you work for or the company you own impact you?
   - How do you feel about yourself when you're at work?
   - Are you invited to make a contribution most days? Describe the contribution you make. Is this the same or different than the contribution you want to make?
   - How do others receive your impact?
   - Is there someone you work with, either a colleague or a customer, who would benefit from hearing about his or her impact on you and your organization?

4. What do you need to do and who do you need to be to create a more positively impactful life?
   - What would you need to change?
   - To let go of?
   - To do or be more of?

Essay 2

You Have to Be Present to Win

You Were Born to Be Brilliant

Our impact is our life's signature. It is the consequence of having been born, lived our lives, and passed on to the next place. It is the marker we leave in place of our lives, and it's what's left over and fossilized. Our impact is the difference we were, the difference we made, and the difference we left. It is not how we will be remembered, but the remembrance itself.

> Our impact is the answer to the question:
> *"What did you come here to do, and are you getting it done?"*

We were born to be brilliant.

Embedded deep within our souls, in the very fiber of our DNA, is our blueprint for greatness. Each one of us has our own unrivaled brand of genius, irrespective of the fact that we may repeatedly forget that. It is as exclusive to us as our thighs, and as quirky as our personalities. Denying our brilliance doesn't make it any duller, ignoring it breeds nothing worth mentioning, and avoiding it brings unnecessary pain, misery, and suffering.

11

> The truth is that our brilliance is in constant search of a place to express itself.

We came into our lives to get something done, something unique to us. Our impact can only be accomplished by us. There is no job sharing. Nor is there a do-over or makeup class. This is it. We are the keeper of our message. If we don't deliver it, it will forever stay in the never-getting-done file. Which would actually be okay, unless you were the one destined to discover the cure for AIDS, world hunger, broken hearts, or global warming. You might, indeed, be fated to give birth to the woman who invents the secret to work/life balance, or how to eliminate multitasking, or keeping white laundry white. Perhaps you signed up for curing adultery, manufacturing zero-calorie healthy chocolate or red wine that melts tummy fat.

You will never know the magnitude of the possibilities of your impact unless you show up in your life. Should we decide to take a pass, every day we will wonder: What if? The agony of that, alone, might inspire us to action. Irrespective of what we came here to do, regardless of our specific life purpose, the only caveat to heed in order to have maximum positive impact is that we have to be present to win. (And no one can win your prize!)

We have a paradoxical relationship with our impact.

> Most of us are not only concerned with making a difference in the world, we are *obsessed* with it, as this is the prime driver of our lives.

Paradoxically, we sometimes minimize the impact we actually have on the world. It can embarrass us. It makes us the center of attention. We may downplay our importance, our footprint, and our value because we have been indoctrinated to be givers, to make a contribution, and to add value wherever we go. We barely give it a second thought because it is so integral to who we are.

> And when we diminish the difference we make, so do the people in our lives.

Then the message we receive, in its most condensed form, is: "Who you are as you are, without any embellishments, without any add-ons, just isn't good enough."

The crazy-making part of this is that I have personally never met an average woman. Not a single one. What I *have* met is too many women who *thought* they were average; felt they were ordinary because someone, or a long strand of someones, taught them they were. Paradoxically, when women *are* acknowledged, when we receive compliments, when accolades flow our way, we can tend to casually dismiss them—which diminishes both the value of what is said *and* who said it to us. No one is winning this game! So let's reframe the way we look at our impact, and let's rewrite the rules by which we play.

> What do you suppose it would take for us to claim our bigness with the same fervor that we sometimes assert our smallness?

Right *now,* for many women, our day-to-day impact means that the laundry is done, the children are bathed, the family is well-fed, and the bills are paid. Our impact comes from something we have done for others, someone we have been for others. This outside-in focus conspires with our insecurities to render us *invisible.* It seems that unless we are smoothing out the wrinkles in others' lives, we are not seen.

What can we do about that? How can we change our visibility factor? We can acknowledge ourselves more! We can appreciate ourselves more! We can see ourselves through a more honest, less self-deprecating, more realistic lens.

> It is our job to have impact, *and* it is our job to be the most enthusiastic champion of the impact we have.

Think about the impact you want to have every day. Think about how you want to feel at the end of the day. Take note of the things that help you to champion yourself. Pay attention when someone says something worth remembering—look in their eyes, hear what they say, feel their words, and repeat them to yourself. Do this for one week, and you'll be impressed with how invincible you feel!

Initiate Impact!

1. What do the people you know tell you about the impact you have in their lives?
2. What excuses do you use for not making a difference in your world?
3. If you were going to do one thing today to shine more brilliantly, what would you do?

Essay 3

Katy Did but We Didn't

If You Want to Have Impact, You Have to Stay in the Game

"Wouldn't it be great if we all had the self-confidence to suck at something!" I said to Katy's dad as we watched our nine-year-old girls play soccer on a soggy Saturday morning.

All eyes were on Katy as she missed a goal once again. Katy was positively lousy at soccer; for the past two years, we had all watched Katy trip and stumble, fumble, and fall. All skinny legs and limbs, this precious child's game was not easy to watch.

Yet game after game Katy picked herself up, retrieved her self-esteem, and gave it another go. Her tenacity was more than admirable—it was award winning! Watching her week after week was a spiritual learning experience for me—one that generated more than a bit of embarrassment. "If only I had the stuff she's made of, what then could I accomplish?" I wondered.

Katy demonstrated remarkable resilience and stamina just by staying in the game when it was evident that others wished she wouldn't. The most courageous thing Katy did was give herself permission to play less than perfectly. Shame on the rest of us for not allowing ourselves to do the same thing!

It's not that Katy didn't notice that she kept messing up. It just didn't bother her like it did us. She didn't have the same judgments or preconceived notions about her performance that we did. Who said "lousy soccer player" is a bad thing?

> This little engine that could simply didn't label her lack of skill and experience as a bad thing, so it didn't stop her from trying again. And again. And again.

To be fair, Katy wasn't really *that* awful at soccer; nor was she a failure or a loser in any sense of the word. In her mind—where it counted most—she'd decided she was a valuable member of her team. That choice and attitude made her a success; it was we adults who needed to get on board with her thinking, not the other way around. Talk about impact!

Katy gave herself permission to play a game she enjoyed, and her only intention was to have fun. Her goal had nothing to do with playing perfectly so, voila, success!

If you're reading about Katy and thinking to yourself, "That's a heartwarming story; but how do *I* do it? How do I get over not being perfect? How do I get over not caring what people think?" then I would say, "High Five Yourself™—you're asking questions that will get you to the answers."

Join me in this brief journey, and imagine a baby who's learning to walk. This little one has been crawling and pulling herself up for quite a while now. One day, she stands on her own, surveying her surroundings with the most delightful air of success about her. She has done it! She has climbed the mountain called, "I am standing on my own, and this is way cool. Is anyone watching?"

At that moment, she lands smack on her padded bottom. The next moment she pulls herself up again. You can see the look on her face that declares that she is going to go for it. If you pay close attention, you'll notice her concentration, as she commands her mind to make her leg move forward as it had done once before. Success! She does the same with the other foot, and then she does it again. She is, by all definitions, walking. "Whoa! Now this is sweet."

The baby belly flops to the floor. Her face crumbles with the loss of dignity. Her little mind conjures up a nonverbal thought akin to, "That's it! I've tried this walking gig and I failed—I was a total loser at it." She vows never to walk again.

> Every time we fail, every time we fall, some little part of us may say, "That's it, I'm done!"

■ ■ ■

When we were born, the life before us was—metaphorically speaking—comparable to Donald Trump's Mar-a-Lago Club, the former estate of Marjorie Meriwether Post. Opportunities were so plentiful that they tripped over one another vying for our attention. "No" was a four-letter word, and "Yes" was our doctrine. Each of the 126-plus rooms offered the perfect environment in which to cultivate our talents, incubate our creativity, and gestate some form of brilliance.

Then life happened to us....

You were two years old and finger-painted on your grandmother's antique wallpaper. You have no idea what the big people said to you, but you knew that it wasn't good. You decided you'd never do that experiment again; and so the door to one of your creative rooms slammed shut.

In kindergarten, Ms. Smith assigned you to draw something cheerful, not realizing that you were going through your dark phase. She sent you to the school counselor. Her disapproval, coupled with your shame at taking your new black crayon for a test drive, has remained with you to this day. Another door to one of your rooms slammed shut.

At the age of 18 you had your first major, heart-hammering, appetite-suppressing, sleep-disrupting love affair—until you found out that he was in love with your best friend. You spent the night ripping through two new diaries, cursing the air that they breathed, while intermittently gorging on every life-inhibiting food in the house. "I will never let myself fall like that again," you swore. Then you threw up. One more door shut—and you nailed this one within an inch of its life.

Many years later, we've forgotten more experiences than we remember. Although we've had scads of memories that were joyous and happy, light and fulfilling, rich and rewarding, we have also closed many doors along the way. We were herded toward places that seemed safe, reliable, secure, practical, professional, long-term, committed, and proven.

> What has that taught us? To look for evidence before we make a choice: To go with the familiar, because God knows what lurks in the darkness of invention.

We've been taught to look for a sure bet, play by the rules, and never, ever, ever, make waves.

We can now see middle age in the vastness before us or in the rearview mirror behind us. When we permit ourselves a morsel of self-indulgence, we look about to notice that we have closed, nailed down, slammed shut, and locked more doors than are now open. We have systematically—though perhaps unconsciously—downsized the Mar-a-Lago estate to a one-room studio apartment. It is no longer beautiful. It will never be spacious. But it's safe, and we know it.

By the time we realized it, we were unwitting prisoners of a safe house of our own design. Fitting in made us feel squeezed out; compliance atrophied to resentment and rebellion; agreement erupted into dissonance; and compromise crept into cheating.

One day something or someone appears on the scene.

> We are reminded of the emotional and mental claustrophobia we've acclimated to, and how cramped we've become in our own lives.

That's it! This neighborhood isn't what it was cracked up to be. We're moving. We venture back to the metaphoric house in which we were born. "No," "can't," "shouldn't," "don't," "why," "never," and all their cousins are tossed out with Monday's trash. Our death-by-mediocrity sentence has been commuted. The freedom we crave waves us over to its side of the street. We follow—exhilarated, alive, and uninhibited.

We are willing, eager even, to relinquish perfection in exchange for happiness. We become more lighthearted in our choices. We throw those proverbial dice, confident in our knowledge that the things that were supposed to bring us contentment snuffed the light out of us instead.

Along comes delightful Katy, just when we need her most. She shows us how life unfettered looks and feels. We get to see freedom, tolerance, acceptance, and the perfection of imperfection. And we ask ourselves, "Isn't it great that I have the self-confidence to suck at something? *Do over!'*

■ ■ ■

If you're wondering how this plays out at work, let's spend a few moments talking about your "real" world—the one in which you think that your boss isn't going to be too happy with you if you're less than perfect.

While it is true that your manager would be delighted (read: relieved that she made the right decision in selecting you for the job) if you maximized your potential, realize that if she is a forward-thinking leader, then perfection is not the goal. A successful manager hired you because of you who are, and the promise she saw in you. If you did your job with 100 percent excellence, then chances are you'd be vying for your boss's job.

Our most daunting task is to build the self-trust and self-confidence required to take healthy risks. If we decide to join in the game then it increases our positive impact and everyone wins.

Initiate Impact!

1. When was a time in your life when you had the courage to suck at something?

2. When was a time when you took yourself out of the game because you couldn't be perfect?

   • Maybe your boss offered to put you in charge of a project but you weren't sure you were up to the task?

3. Is there a situation at work right now where you're abdicating your opportunity to have impact because you aren't the best player on the field?

Essay 4

I Was Absent That Day

What Happens When You Don't Have Impact

Nothing.

Okay, actually, something *does* happen:

- Depression (see Essay #18)
- Anxiety (see Essay #18)
- Fear (see Essay #20)

Part Two

Why Is Impact Important?

Essay 5

For God's Sake

Our Life Purpose Is the Essence of Our Impact and Invincibility

217 million	Pages of hits for the search term "life purpose" on msn.com
101 million	Pages of hits for the search term "spiritual" on Google
50 million	People who identify as SBNR (spiritual but not religious)
30 million	Copies sold of Rick Warren's *The Purpose Driven Life*
3.6 million	People who self-describe as atheist or agnostic
3.5 million	Copies sold of Eckhart Tolle's *A New Earth: Awakening to Your Life's Purpose* in just one month after Oprah recommended it
4,300	Faith groups around the world
92%	People who believe in God and/or a universal spirit
89%	People who believe in God
60%	People who pray at least once a day
40%	People who attend services every week
6%	People to whom religion is unimportant

based on American population

■ ■ ■

God is at the top of *my* agenda. Actually, God *is* my agenda.

My work is not to argue the politics of religion, or to debate whether God actually exists. I trust that you will negotiate the relationship between you and Him as it best serves you. I don't have an agenda as to what *you* call God. I experience God as a universal life force, an energy that permeates all things. A seed of that same divine energy, a virtual microcosm, lives, grows, and thrives within all of us. We can no more separate ourselves from the source than we can take the white off rice.

> The purpose of our lifetime, *"the why behind the what"* we do, is to discover the God within us and to make it reality—to actualize His intention for us.

Our life purpose is the vehicle by which we can *become* the God within us, and fulfill the promise that this implies. This is the essence of impact and invincibility.

For those who don't embrace the term *God,* I would offer this: There is a power, a force, an energy, a spirit, that connects all things to one another. While it is greater than each of us, we are, nonetheless, *of* it. See if that definition works for you; if not, come up with a personal statement of your own, one that resonates deeply for you.

A concrete example of this abstraction would be to picture yourself standing at the ocean's shore. You hold a glass that you fill with seawater; and while the water in the glass is *from* the ocean, it is not *the* ocean. Obviously, the ocean is far too large to fit into the glass. Yet what is in the glass is a tiny piece of vastness—a symbolic representation of it.

So it is with God and us. Since all of God cannot be contained within our body, a virtual seed of that energy is harbored within us as a representation of all that is God. Being "on purpose" is the closest to God we will ever get. Our heart is home to this symbol of God. It is from the heart that true leaders are born. It is from our God-self that we cultivate our impact. There are many names for this energy and although it's my personal preference to call it God, you might call it her/him:

- Allah
- The Omnipresent
- Supreme Being
- Buddha
- Greater Light
- God
- God-Self
- Higher power
- Hunch
- Inner Light
- Inner Wisdom
- Instinct
- Intuition
- Jesus Christ
- Light that I am
- Source
- Spirit
- Spiritual Self
- The Divine
- The Universe
- Universal Energy
- The Truth
- _____

The choice is personal; and it is yours, of course. I use various names throughout this book. What matters most is that you ponder the notion that you are a part of something greater than yourself; and that you and only you have the personal power to access it, realize its potential, and fulfill its destiny.

Our greatest desire is to *know* our God-Self and to be one with it; not to believe in it, but to know it with the same assuredness that we know the color of our eyes. Why? Because that's how we've been designed! Just as we've been deep-wired to seek food when we're hungry and to sleep when we're tired, we are permanently programmed to seek wholeness and completion at the spiritual and emotional level. Spiritually speaking, The Law of Identification states that "the thing has to become itself." So the acorn has to become the oak tree. We are destined to become more of who *we* are meant to be, more of our God-Self.

A deep hunger pulses in the soul of a seeker; and these days we're a ravenous society. Spiritually ravenous, truth be told. Every significant thing we do is targeted by this spiritual craving. Consciously and un-consciously, we solicit emotional experiences as a way to engage with that seed of God within us, similar to the way a child experiments with attention-getting behavior with a parent. That engagement anchors us to God when we're in the middle of a personal storm. That connected-ness with our soul keeps us grounded in times of elation. That reliance on our core self keeps us tethered to our life purpose when distractions would dissuade us.

> *"It is who we become as a result of the experience, not the experience itself, which is most valuable."*
> —Nancy D. Solomon

The events of our lives may be joyous, passionate, loving, and happy; or they may be occasions of fear, anger, resentment, pain, and all their dark and distant relatives. No matter, the value is the same: to turn inward so that we can become one with the greater light within us, and be congruent with our spiritual selves. Repeatedly I see some people create struggle just to bring themselves closer to God. Every time I've done that I've ended up wondering why I didn't just go straight to God in the first place—why I had to create drama as an excuse to go there.

On a practical level, you may be saying to yourself, "That's crazy! I didn't want to break up with my lover." "I didn't choose to be laid off." "It wasn't my idea to lose my 401k in this economic debacle we're going through!" Wasn't it?

In two words: yes and no.

While we may not have had a hand in creating the specific event, we *are* accountable for our reaction to the event. And that reaction, to be very clear, is intricately tied to the requisite emotional and spiritual experiences we need to satisfy our life purpose.

What this correctly implies is that we unwittingly search for experiences that will provide us with the emotional and spiritual repertoire that is appropriate to our specific life purpose and journey (see Essay #6).

Sometimes we say that our hearts "tug" at us; when we feel the intuitive urge to go in one direction instead of another, our hunches override our minds, and it feels like we are being pushed in a direction we had no thought of following. This is our GPS (God Positioning System) guiding us back to our life purpose. Being at one with The

Universe is our natural state. Again, it may not be everyone's definition of normal, but it is natural.

You may be thinking to yourself, "Okay, but what does this have to do with my impact?" Everything!

■ ■ ■

> The universal currency of spirit is emotion.

Consider this: Every human being experiences emotion. It is one of the few things common to all people. The physical event is transitory, and its memory fades with time, but the emotion that accompanied the event is sustained. Not certain this is valid for you? Think back, right now, on any event in your entire life; and don't edit. Now recall the emotion filed away with that experience.

Experience_____

Emotion_____

> We do what we do because of the way it makes us feel.

Do you see how powerful that is? You may not remember the specifics of the event, but you can be assured that you can recall how you felt. Why is that? We seek experiences primarily for the emotions that are a consequence of them. Events are a centrifuge for our values, which translate to feelings. Your 98-year-old neighbor did not buy that little red Corvette because it gets great gas mileage; he bought it because of the way it makes him feel. Similarly, you didn't take that job for the salary alone. You took it because of your expectation about how you would feel with that particular set of responsibilities, *and* because of how that salary would make you feel about yourself. You married your spouse because of how you felt when you were with him or her. You bought those 4-inch heels because of the way you felt when you tried them on. You gave up the object of your addiction because you didn't like the way it made you feel about yourself.

Striking a cord? Here's an example.

I *save money* because I want to feel *safe*.

I took a *job* with a large company because I want to feel *secure*.

I *married my husband* because I want to feel *stable*.

Let's personalize this for you.

PART I

Take three examples from your own life.

I _____ because I want to feel _____.

I _____ because I want to feel _____.

I _____ because I want to feel _____.

PART II

Take a look at your pattern(s) and note the common theme(s). As you go through this exercise, you'll notice that certain motivators are stronger than others. You'll see patterns that, up until now, you might have assigned a negative label. For instance, "I'm neurotic." "I go from one addiction to the next." "I keep getting into relationships with unavailable people." "I will do anything to avoid change."

A common theme in my life is: _____

A common theme in my life is: _____

A common theme in my life is: _____

What you will discover is that these patterns have nothing to do with "what's wrong with you" and everything to do with *what's right with you.*

Your life's experiences are not only *not random*; they are spiritually deliberate and *the* most significant component for you to have impact. These themes connect the dotted line between you and your life purpose and, therefore, between you and your impact. Instead of looking at your patterns through a lens called "I'm damaged," look at them through a lens called "I'm getting closer to my God-Self" or "This is perfect" or "I sure got clear on what I don't want."

Living our life from a vantage point of what's right with us helps us focus on our brilliance, on the contribution we are, on our gifts and talents, and on the things that make us feel happiest and most joyful. There are few opportunities more personally powerful than being able to reframe every event of our life as something that was designed to support us, encourage us, and get us closer to our divine source.

Your ability to reframe your experiences in this way will make you invincible.

Initiate Impact!

1. What are some common themes in your life?
  ◆ How do they carry over into your work?
2. How do these themes impact your life?
3. How do these themes impact your relationships?
4. What's *right* with you?

Essay 6

The Why Behind the What

The Impact Cycle

Congratulations! You have finally arrived in the life you spent 20-odd years in school preparing for. You have checked off a number of important life to-dos, you've had a variety of both great and forgettable experiences, and, lately you've found yourself wondering what you're doing and why you're doing it.

How *did* you get from "I love my job!" to "My job is just okay, I don't know how to make it better—or even if it's what I want to be doing!" Great questions deserve powerful answers!

Obviously you know *what* you do in your life; it's the profession you chose or the one that chose you. Your *what* could be a lawyer, manager, teacher, or fitness trainer. I'm going to apologize, in advance, for saying this: "So what!" That's right, "So what!"

Your *what* is not essential to the achievement of your success, the actualization of your life purpose, or the enhancement of your relationship with your inner wisdom, with God. It is merely your vehicle—even though, culturally, your *what* likely defines you.

The *imperative* is for you to have a thorough and complete understanding of "*why you do what you do.*" The *why* is the emotional and spiritual experience your life is being called to, it is your life purpose, and it is why you are here to begin with. See Figure 6.1.

32

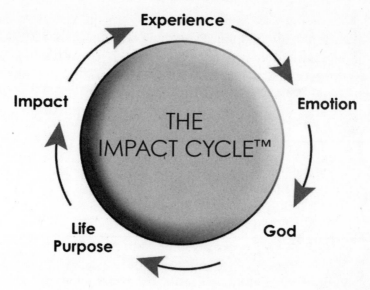

FIGURE 6.1   The Impact Cycle summarizes the relationship between what we do and why we do it.

Our emotions, as the universal currency of spirit (see Essay #5), are the means by which we connect to God, to the Universe. They are also the conduit to the greater light within us, to our God-self. Emotions are the most efficient language for communication between two people, or between people and an enterprise. Prayer is activated by the emotions assigned to it.

1. We have a life experience for its emotional content.
2. The emotions provide an opportunity for us to go within, and to become more emotionally and spiritually intimate with ourselves.
3. This self-awareness stimulates our inner wisdom, our God-Self, and helps us to access our own brand of spirituality. That spirituality has a direct and profound correlation to our life purpose (which is what we came here to do).
4. When we are fulfilling our life purpose, when we are "getting it done," we create positive impact.
5. The cycle begins again with the next experience.

Are you seeing the pattern here? Once again, emotions are the universal currency of the spirit. Everything we do, as spiritual humans, is for the emotional experience, which segues to God, which segues to our life purpose, which, when all is said and done, results in our impact.

> "We seek the life experiences we do, solely for the emotional value they provide."
> —Nancy D. Solomon

The value of our emotions cannot be overemphasized just as the emotional value of an experience cannot be exaggerated. The things that are most alive for us are those that provide us with the most vibrant emotional payoff (whether positive or negative), and an equal measure of spiritual *ahas*.

Think about it for a minute. What you do doesn't matter. Where you do it doesn't matter. How you do it doesn't even matter. *Why you do it and that you do it is all that really counts!* Consider this: If the ultimate objective of your life's journey is a specific emotional and spiritual adventure, then you can do any job, anywhere in the world, for any amount of money, as long as you are having that emotional and spiritual experience—the one that aligns with your life purpose. What's the implication of this? What happens in our lives when we adopt this perspective? The doors to global opportunity fly open! Instead of one or two jobs or career moves to apply for, there are literally hundreds that can help us satisfy the emotional outcome we're seeking. Remember— you'll no longer be looking for a job, you'll be pursuing an emotional and spiritual lifestyle.

When you recall people who have had an impact on you, do you remember what they did, or do you remember how you felt about what they did and how you felt about them? Exactly! The feelings will *always* have precedence over the event. Why? *Because* we are emotion-seeking creatures, first and foremost: Any conversation to the contrary has gone the way of girdles and *The Ed Sullivan Show.*

■ ■ ■

> *"The journey of our lives is about becoming who we were meant to be. The experiences of our lives are the vehicles that get us there."*
> —Nancy D. Solomon

What happens if we ignore, deny, or minimize the spirit within us? It's common practice to attempt to fill that void with something other than Divine energy. We may resort to eating out of control, drinking beyond our limits, or exercising to the point of utter depletion. We form these habits with the hope that the excesses will drown out our inner voice. And as we form our habits, our habits form us. I've never met a person for whom this has worked, nor have I met anyone whose meal or workout brought the same inner peace, happiness, or life fulfillment that accompanies God.

There are some people who claim that there's no place for God in business. I think we haven't any business being anywhere without God. I've noticed in my coaching business that people come to me only on rare occasion because they lack the strategic or tactical skills to excel at their jobs. For the most part, maybe 90 to 95 percent of the time, people contact me because of how they *feel* in their jobs—not what they are doing, but how they feel about what they are doing. These people are off purpose. My job is to assist them to see that, and to give them the roadmap back to their personal paths.

Let's visit with Laurie, who was a senior executive for one of the nation's largest telecommunications companies. Although she was passionate about her job, and had recently broken all sales records when she won an eight-figure contract for her company, Laurie was neither content nor fully happy. Married to a man whom she adored, the two had been unable to have children in the 10 years they'd been married, and Laurie was feeling quite disappointed about it.

Laurie spent the first few months in coaching exploring why she was doing what she was doing. She realized that she felt safer working 70 hours a week than she did at the prospect of becoming a mother; her own mother had suffered from mental illness and Laurie's childhood was an endless stream of drama.

Laurie discovered that the true source of her dissonance was between her desire to have a child and her fear of doing so. Instead of facing this head-on, Laurie had lost herself in work that was a long emotional distance from parenthood. The coaching work Laurie did revealed that her life purpose was 'care-giving.' It made perfect sense, having been the caregiver of her mother throughout her youth, and as the executive in charge of her company's entire sales force: Both allowed her to combine her business acumen with her emotional intelligence. No wonder she'd excelled! There was a time in her life when Laurie's job fulfilled her life purpose of care taking. But that time had long passed and her inner wisdom was now calling her to a more deeply satisfying spiritual expression of her "why behind her what."

Laurie spent months trying to identify the wisdom of her inner voice. What did that part of her support? Her friends thought she was insane to even contemplate leaving a monthly compensation package that rivaled their yearly wages. Should she listen to them?

But Laurie knew, deep in her heart, that her job was off-purpose for her; her heart was calling her to motherhood and the more she ignored it, the longer hours she put in at the office. I gave Laurie the coaching assignment to keep her work hours to 50 per week for one month. I suggested to her that if she momentarily stopped hiding, the truth would reveal itself.

Let's track Laurie's trip around the Impact Cycle.

Experience	Something was off, or at least, not on, in her life: Dissonance and upset with her 'ideal' job.
Emotion	Fear of becoming a mother collided with her fear of not becoming a mother.

God   She went within her spiritual self and prayed and
               meditated about what she needed to know about her
               dilemma. This re-ignited her spiritual life and her deep
               belief in God—something she'd become removed from
               over the years.
Life Purpose   She discovered that her life purpose is 'care taking' but
               the vehicle she was using to implement it wasn't the
               right one for that time in her life.

What happened? Some of you will frame this as a random occurrence in a serendipitous world. Others will likely agree that as soon as
Laurie got clear, and was able to articulate her true desires, the universe
synchronized with her plans and gave her what she wanted and needed
to fulfill her life purpose.

One evening, out of the blue, Laurie and her husband received a call
about a teenage mom in her eighth month of pregnancy. Were Laurie
and her husband interested in adopting? Well, they were and they did!
And surprise—not six months later the family received another call from
yet another agency and, as of today, Laurie and her husband now have
two small children, only six months apart.

Impact   Laurie became a mother, twice over!

Although she had been initially torn about what to do with her career.
Laurie's two babies made the decision crystal clear for her. Ecstatic
about listening to her heart, and having found her path, Laurie is now
a stay-at-home mom. When strangers ask about the babies' ages, she
giggles and gleefully credits God.

Initiate Impact!

 1. What emotional experiences have you repeatedly had through-
    out your life?
 2. How do these experiences impact your life? Your work?
 3. Do you know *why you do what you do*—your life purpose?
    ◆ How does knowing your purpose influence your life?
    ◆ If you don't know your purpose, what do you imagine would
      be different in your life if you did?

Essay 7

When Your Life Calls, Answer It!

Your Purpose Is Your Life's Agenda

There are many things we do just for the heck of it. Life should not be one of them.

We are all born with a life purpose, a raison d'être. Just as we go to the bakery intending to buy bread, and we go to school intending to be educated, we arrive in this lifetime with the sole objective of fulfilling our life purpose. Our purpose is our life's agenda, our assignment as human beings; it is the goal around which the rest of our lives are structured. It is deep wired into our spiritual, emotional, mental, and physical bodies; it functions as a homing device, pre-programmed to guide us back to our most authentic, divine Self.

Just as an animal might be implanted with a microchip to track its journey and bring it home when it's lost, our purpose serves as a GPS—or, as I like to call it, a God Positioning System—of sort, guiding us through our lives and keeping us on our path. The absence or suspension of our conscious awareness of our life purpose—or the ways in which we stray from home—will trigger an internal signal to help us course-correct. This schema is constructed in such a fashion that we will be reminded of who we are whenever we forget; something that can be a fairly frequent occurrence.

> Our GPS is similar to a compass whose needle perpetually points to our potential for impact.

We arrived in our lives to fulfill a specific once-in-a-lifetime job; that job is our purpose, our promise, our agreement, and our commitment. We made this vow with God before we were born. Now that we're here, we don't get to renegotiate the deal. There's no bartering for one we think we'd like better and no backsies are permitted. No two jobs are identical, so if we don't fill the position, it will remain vacant for eternity. No one else can do our job for us and no spiritual job sharing is permitted. Our purpose remains the same over the course of our entire lifetime.

Although our life's commitments were agreed upon before we entered this incarnation, how we choose to manage them is subject to the conscious choices we make *now*. The plaster may have been poured, but it has yet to dry; we can consciously choose the impression we will leave in it—which is our impact. Our life purpose evolves as we do, matching our growth step for step. As we mature, it expands. It also provides a little nudge from behind if we become complacent for too long.

> You cannot overestimate the value of knowing your life purpose. *Note:* Knowing your life purpose is your 100 percent money back guarantee that you'll have impact.

And that's not all. Consider this: We don't have just one life purpose, we actually have two—a *global purpose* and a *personal purpose*. And although each one is distinct in its own right, the two dovetail seamlessly throughout our lives. Our *personal purpose* is what we came into our lives to accomplish exclusively for ourselves in order to be able to, ultimately, fulfill our global purpose. Our *global purpose* is what we came to contribute to the other six billion people in the world. This is discussed further in Essay #8.

■ ■ ■

Our purpose is the mega message of our lives, the overarching theme by which we live. Knowing and living our purpose gives absolute and complete meaning to everything in our world. It is the foundation on which all our success depends and, as such, its fulfillment is imperative for our happiness and life contentment; this pertains equally to the pursuit of a new career, improvement in our work performance, the enhancement of our parenting skills, and so on. Immutable and enduring, our life purpose is the driving force behind every significant thing in our life that we do, regardless of whether or not that is our intent.

> It is not only central to who we are; at every level our purpose *is* who we are.

Living on purpose inspires us, and compels us to translate our potential into something substantive; therein lies the impact of our actions. Although our lives will never be without bumps and bruises or rejections and failures, knowing the larger picture, and having a 10,000-foot view, provides us with the perspective to see beyond immediate circumstances and events. After all, there is nothing like a little altitude to motivate us to keep plowing through the waist-high mud of life.

(Refusal to believe that you have a life purpose doesn't make it any less true, just as a disbelief in gravity doesn't prevent you from falling. This applies equally to you, if you are nihilistic by nature: Your function may simply be to provide contrast to those of us who have spiritual and moral principles by which we live.)

Once we are clear about what our life purpose is, life becomes much simpler (although not necessarily easier) for us. We're able to gain a sense of perspective, direction, and guidance in our decision-making process, irrespective of the size of those decisions.

In an ideal scenario, those things that are "on purpose" are assigned to our to-do list, and those things that don't purposefully fit are unceremoniously discarded.

Much like pregnancy—a condition in which you either are, or you're not, without middle ground—we are either on purpose or off purpose. There is no gradation with which to quibble.

Let's say, for example, that your life purpose is connection. Anything involving your ability to connect would provide you with a sense of reason. That might include the connection of people, of groups, of businesses, of ideas, such as:

- Relationship building (connecting with an individual)
- Meditating (connecting with yourself)
- A referral-based business (connecting b2b)
- Mediation (connecting opposing parties), etc.

Let's say that an opportunity presents itself in which you realize there will be little occasion for you to utilize your talent for connection. There's a fairly good chance that, should you decide to proceed anyway, it will either not utilize your precious time; or it may not turn out well and you'll wish you'd never committed.

Why am I making such a big deal of your life purpose? Because there is no deal that's bigger! Period.

As the virtual operating system of our life, it is impossible to simultaneously be powerful and be off purpose. It is only when we are *on purpose* that our power is released. Think of a garden hose with several tight knots and kinks in it. The water may trickle through, but the flow is severely restricted by those knots, making a surge not possible. This is what happens to us when we're unaware of our objective in life.

It's worth mentioning that it *is* possible to be off purpose and have a perfectly fine life. But fine is not my aim; and I sure hope that it's not yours either. There's no way of knowing the exact numbers, but my guess would be that 90 to 95 percent of the general population is either living off purpose right now, or has been at some point in their lives. That is simply the human condition, to say nothing of the fact that parts of our culture are relatively unconscious and disengaged and seem invested in staying that way.

> You will likely find, as my clients have, that when you choose to include off-purpose items on your agenda (perhaps your ego weighed in on the decision?), life becomes more complicated, chaotic, and confusing, much like a socially acceptable form of hell.

■ ■ ■

In the name of transparency (and to accentuate this point), I am about to share with you the single most humiliating experience of my entire professional career. My primary motive, in case you're wondering, is somewhat self-serving. After thinking a great deal about the risk that accompanies this type of exposure, I decided—having already completely and publicly mortified myself—that I might as well make certain it wasn't for nothing. In other words, I didn't want this opportunity to go to waste; if by sharing my experience I could save you an equal measure of humiliation, I decided I should do so.

It was in the early 1990s, and I had recently moved to the northwestern United States. Having run out of time, money, and ideas to launch my new career, I was—to put it delicately—eager to get some business. Okay, so maybe I was desperate the day I agreed to do something I had absolutely no business doing—speak to a group of 100 women about the fishing industry. Yes, the fishing industry.

Now, if you're sitting there thinking, "Wait a minute. Nancy doesn't talk about the fishing industry. Nancy talks about empowerment, courage, leadership, retention, and impact," – well, that would be exactly right! Therein lay the problem: Accepting this assignment was the epitome of foolishness, and an event that I have yet—and hope never—to forget (hopefully precluding its repetition).

I might mention at this juncture that this presentation was to be given gratis, as I was promised it would be great exposure. The exposure I got, however, was not the kind that I could use to my advantage. (You'll see why shortly.)

Only a few weeks from the scheduled event, I began researching the fishing industry, a topic about which I knew absolutely nothing (excluding cooking it and deveining shrimp). In fact, I had as much to learn about my topic as I did about speaking: I checked out a few books from the library on how to actually give a speech; since that, too, had only recently been added to my repertoire of talents.

I put together a presentation of sorts and, on the appointed day, headed over to the restaurant where the event was taking place. I dragged along my then-boyfriend so that he could video the entire production for my demo tape (ignorance is indeed blissful). I am slapping my forehead as I recount this.

So there I was, minutes before show time; when I realized, in a flash of blinding brilliance, that I had no idea what the @%&%X* I was doing there—and that, in just a moment or two, 100 other people would be wondering as well. I kid you not when I confess that as I stood in the restroom (sweat pouring down my armpits, pooling at the waistband of my skirt as my knees loudly knocked together), I calculated what it would take to run out of the door and throw myself in front of a speeding truck without incurring permanent body damage. Really.

I approached the podium robotically—sweat still pouring, knees still knocking—and gave my speech. The second I left the riser, I could not have told you one thing I had said during that hour. Amnesia erased any recall, save my memory of the only person who volunteered during Q & A—an inebriated man who had wandered in off the street. I was too nervous to notice that he didn't belong there, and I actually answered his incoherent question (nobody makes this stuff up). Several women told me I did a great job: Either they weren't listening, or they were willing to do anything to help me save face.

I returned home with the boyfriend and drank my weight in wine.

The following day, I called the client who had invited me to speak. In the most unattractive and undiplomatic rant, she shared her thoughts about my presentation. None of what she said is fit to print.

Stop laughing! Sounds pathetic, doesn't it? If at all possible, the actual experience was even worse than my description of it! The word "cataclysmic" comes to mind. To this day, I cannot drive past that restaurant without my stomach flipping over with angst, so traumatic to me was this event.

What did I learn? First, never, ever, *ever*, agree to do anything incongruent with your life purpose; for any reason or for any amount of money. Know what your purpose is, and never stray from it. I'm serious!

> Second, desperation brings more of the same; anything we do out of ego (fear, scarcity, lack, anger, etc.) will, decidedly not work. So don't do it.

Initiate Impact

1. What parts of your life are working smoothly right now?
2. Where are you on purpose in your life?
   - What is the impact you're having in these areas?
3. Where does your life need to get back on track?
   - How will you accomplish that?
4. When you've been off purpose in your life, what have you noticed about yourself?
   - About your life?
   - What have others noticed about you?

Essay 8

Brand You

Your Brand Is Your Life Purpose

Baryshnikov. Streisand. Oprah. Branson. Streep. Obama.

In alignment; in contribution; on purpose. All these people epitomize their fields and demonstrate their gifts in an unforgettable, influential, and iconic fashion. They not only *do* their jobs, they *are* their jobs. The mere mention of their names instantaneously brings their brand to the forefront of our minds, and makes the important point that:

> Our brand is our life purpose.

To be exact: our brand is the physical, mental, emotional, and spiritual *manifestation* of our life purpose. It's what we *literally* stand for—the values and actions that others associate with us. Want to know what someone's life purpose is? Articulate their brand.

Life purpose is at the heart of every hugely successful endeavor. Take another look at those names at the beginning of this essay; not an ambiguous or mediocre thing about any of them. Neither is there anything ordinary about you when you are on purpose and living your passion. The most accomplished people bring a true sense of purpose

45

to their work. Yes, they want to make a living, *and* they approach their everyday business with higher goals in mind—to contribute, educate, help people become financially sound, serve the community, and so much more. They love what they do, and it is by no means just about the money.

Purpose is also at the heart of most social and cultural movements. The human potential movement, personal empowerment programs, effectiveness training, and both religious and spiritual disciplines are built on the principles of life purpose.

It occurs to me that, 100 years from now, Bill Gates will not necessarily be remembered for founding Microsoft. Our great, great grandchildren may not realize his part in revolutionizing the high tech industry, and the ensuing impact that has on world globalization. What *will* be written in the history books is that the Gates Foundation helps to heal the world of many of its more devastating diseases such as malaria and HIV/AIDS, and tuberculosis. He will be lauded for the global development programs that increase opportunities for developing nations to ameliorate hunger and poverty. Right here in the United States, future generations will know him as the man whose non-profit makes remarkable progress improving the public education system, and insuring that students are appropriately prepared for post-secondary education.

Think about this: Bill Gates's life purpose is not bigger, better, or more important than yours. He is *just* doing his job. Perhaps the only thing that differentiates him from many of us is the degree to which he takes his purpose seriously, and the extent to which he chooses to materialize it: Obviously his scale is exponentially bigger than many and, therefore, so is his impact.

Our personal brand is a powerful, clear, positive idea that comes to mind whenever other people think of us.

Our friends, colleagues and family know our personal brand just by knowing us. We can't fudge this; it's authentic, and it endures the test of time—or it's not our personal brand.

Our personal brand is the promise of the value people will receive by spending time with us. It tells prospective clients what they can expect when they do business with us, and that is why it's so commercially powerful. Those of us who either "own" a piece of business within an organization or actually own the organization are selling our *contribution*, not our job, to our clients or customers.

Only when we're aware of our purpose can we actually begin to "*get it done.*" If we don't know what our life purpose is, we won't be able to lead our life; we'll merely follow it around. Then nothing of much worth gets done, and we take up room more than we have impact. When we live our purpose, when our business is an extension of that purpose, and when the highest goal of our business aligns with that purpose, then this is another demonstration of our personal brand.

So where do you begin? What do you do to create and develop your personal brand? Nothing. You don't have to *do* anything: Be the most passionate, the most capable, the most authentic you that you can possibly be. This takes no small amount of courage! You get to be your brand with your family, in your community, and at work. You get to lead from the brand you are, wherever you are. Your brand is a straight shot to your invincibility, because it is who you are at your purest.

■ ■ ■

> *"Our life is our own best testimonial."*
> —Nancy D. Solomon

In order to grasp any concept, we must also know its contrast. For example, if we want to know what up means, we need to experience down. If we want to know what right means, we need to experience left. If we want to know what abundance means, knowing scarcity would be helpful to us. Likewise, if we want to know what it means to be powerful, a functional experience of disempowerment will be just the catalyst that we need for our learning.

Irrespective of what our purpose is, in order "get it done" during our lifetime, we must experience the entire spectrum of that purpose: from its dark point straight through all the variations of gray, right to the lightest version of it. This is particularly pertinent with regard to our personal purpose.

Here's a concrete example of the theory: If your personal purpose is power, then you may also dance many rounds with disempowerment, misuse of power, abuse of power, as well as empowerment throughout your lifetime. In other words, we don't just get to do the good stuff, we don't just get to look good to the world; we get to muck around in the mud so that we have a full, rich, and complete adventure with our purpose.

A concentrated number of these contrasting experiences may occur from our youth through our mid-thirties. We encounter random people, relationships, family dynamics, and colleagues in which every possible scenario involving power is presented to us. Consider this your very own customized learning lab. Think about it—what better way is there to learn to take full responsibility for our personal power than to be born into a family that renders us powerless every step of the way?

> The intention of our purpose is *always* to show us how powerful we are, where our potential lies, and how to have the maximum positive impact.

In order to drive this home—to emphasize its significance in our lives—let's return to that hypothetical person whose personal purpose is power. This same person might have leadership as her global purpose. The relationship between all the facets of power and all the facets of leadership are obvious, aren't they? Can you imagine the number of configurations possible between these two ideas, given the multiple aspects each one has? It's practically incalculable, isn't it, given the range of possibilities?

Does it now make sense that before we can have impact in the area of leadership (our global purpose), we would first need to have a comprehensive working understanding of our relationship with our personal power? And when we have relative mastery of our personal power, only then would we be prepared to integrate it with the vastness of leadership theory, and take that myriad of possibilities out into the world?

Now let's pull this all together, shall we?

Your personal purpose belongs exclusively to you. You cannot cram yourself into someone else's purpose *or* someone else's idea of your purpose and expect to be happy and successful. If, for a nanosecond, you think that you're the exception to this construct, please read Essay #7 in which I offer myself up as the poster child for what happens when we walk someone else's path instead of our own.

Are *your* goals *your* own?

Just as we influence life, life influences us. That reciprocity can confuse the heck out of us when we're not yet clear on what our life purpose is and have yet to define our personal brand. Exposure to ideas from our family of origin, society, the media, our peers, and others can interfere with the evolution of our own goals and aspirations; and it can become quite the challenge to distinguish between what we want for ourselves and what others want for us.

It is not uncommon to get swept up in the momentum of the dreams of those who love us. As unintentional as this outcome is on their part, it is our responsibility to determine our future. To blame them for unduly influencing us is akin to blaming the shoe that gave us a blister.

The preponderance of goals that others want for us and that we have learned to want for ourselves, are external in nature: the house, job, money, relationship, vacation, whatever. These culturally sanctioned goals are impermanent. The job can be made redundant. The vacation is over. The relationship can end in divorce court. The money can be lost in the market. All these aspirations depended on our having or doing something.

The goals that perennially sustain us, on the other hand, are the internal ones. They are, not incidentally, the identical ones that cultivate our life purpose. Internal goals—or, as I prefer to call them, ultimate goals—are grounded in our spiritual and/ or emotional desires. Fulfilling these goals rewards us with coveted feelings such as peace, love, joy, contentment, balance, and so on.

Just as our purpose is the "why behind the what" in our lives, an internal goal is the goal behind the goal. Perhaps we truly want that vacation so that we can be *relaxed*; or we want that relationship so we can be *happy*; or we want that job so we can be *successful*; all of which will eventually help us to be *content*.

> What I find to be true is that when we stop to ask ourselves why we want what we want, we discover that it may not actually be "the thing" that we want, but the feeling that the thing elicits in us that is our primary goal.

Ask yourself *why* you want what you want.

- What is the goal behind your goal?
- What emotions do you value?
- What spiritual state do you seek?
- Did someone tell you that having a six-bedroom house would make you look as though you're successful?
- Were you taught that a large diamond ring meant that he loved you more than if the ring were small?
- Is the corner office your idea of having made it, or is that simply something you heard that you should want?

It is neither my job nor my desire to discourage you from setting material goals. I love my things as much as the next person does. Like many of you, I have a long list of written objectives I have every intention of achieving. So please, ladies—understand that I'm not telling you to get rid of your ambitions, or downsize your shopping list.

Read these words as encouragement to raise your expectations, to elevate your ambition, and increase your desire to *get more of what you want by being more of who you are.*

Ponder this: When you fantasize about the perfect home, in the perfect neighborhood, in the perfect city, there are only a finite number of locations that will satisfy your mental picture. However, if your goal behind your goal is to be happy, content, safe, and balanced, then there are a plethora of places that might provide that emotional experience. The universe is simply waiting for you to reach that realization so that it can conspire with your greater good to provide you with what you desire.

And if you want *both* the external and internal goals, the more power to you! Start with the internal, start with the emotional feeling, start with the spiritual experience. Why? Because wherever you go, there you are! And no one—and nothing—can take that from you.

Initiate Impact!

1. In clear concise language, write down your personal brand.
2. How does your brand impact your relationship with your work?
3. If you aren't clear about your brand, ask three people who know you well to define your brand for you (i.e., how do they experience you?)
4. Make a list of your internal goals and another list of your external goals
   - What is the pattern or theme that links the two?
   - What, if anything, would you need to change to be more on purpose in your life?

Essay 9

There Are No Victims[1]

The Power of Choice

Janine was laid off as vice president of a community bank when the industry first began to soften. Janine is a very bright, easy-to-work-with people-person who had advanced quickly in her field. She was headed for great things—and then her career slammed head-on into a failing economy.

Though she was a banker who "should" have known better, that rainy day for which she'd saved had turned out to be monsoon season. She was caught with a sizable negative cash flow that soon had her wallowing in debt. Try as she might, she simply couldn't get a job at or even near the level at which she had previously performed. After six months, Janine was, quite literally, willing to do *anything* to be working again.

One rainy afternoon, a friend of a friend of a friend called to tell her about a job in advertising that would be perfect for her; the only caveat was that Janine had to get to the interview within an hour's time. The job had been posted the week before, they'd just had an interviewee cancel, and they urgently needed to fill the position. Ecstatic for the

---

[1]Unfortunately, there are millions of women all over the world who are victims, solely because of their gender. The title of this essay *does not* refer to those women—to them we send much love. "There are no victims" refers to the circumstances when we have viable *choices* as to whether to hold the perspective of victim, or that of invincible.

opportunity Janine raced to get dressed, gathered her portfolio, and was on her way.

Five minutes into the drive, just as she was about to exit the highway into downtown Seattle, her car stalled. Then stopped. Permanently. Oh, no. "What now!" Janine cried. She mentally reviewed her circumstances: no job, no money, no confidence—and nine minutes to get to her interview in the pouring rain without a car. To complicate matters even further, she'd forgotten her cell phone in her rush to be on time.

With her car parked on the narrow shoulder, Janine ran down the list of options she had. Run through the rain; walk through the rain; and pray that she'd safely get off the highway. What would she tell her prospective boss?

The knock on her window scared her so much that she gasped out loud. She'd been so wrapped up in her dilemma that she hadn't seen the well-dressed man who had driven up in a late-model Mercedes and approached her car, umbrella in hand. He looked safe enough, Janine thought; so she rolled down her window and, sobbing, told him of her situation. Without hesitating, he handed her the cell phone in his pocket and suggested that she contact her interviewer to tell her she'd possibly be a few minutes late. The man offered to take her to her interview and call a tow truck. Disregarding childhood admonishments not to get into a car with a stranger, Janine accepted his gracious offer.

Four minutes later, they pulled up in front of the building for Janine's scheduled interview. She was on time. And she got the job!

What came into your mind as you read Janine's story? Did you think she was a flake? Or inept, because she couldn't even get to a job interview without upset and drama? Did you wonder if *this* is why she'd been laid off? Did you think that she had an unconscious desire to fail or to sabotage herself? Did you conclude that she was disempowered?

Or . . .

Did you think she was simply amazing and personally powerful because, despite the seeming desperation of her situation, she was able to "magically" create what she needed in that moment of crisis—a safe ride, a cell phone, and a tow truck? What feelings did this evoke for you? What were your thoughts and judgments?

Whatever your opinion was about Janine's situation is exactly what you'd think of yourself in similar circumstances—when you're under stress or when your self-confidence is on vacation. As we discussed in Essay #29: *"we see life as we are,"* through whatever lens we choose. And *choose* is the operative word here.

> Power—like courage, purpose, impact, and invincibility—is a choice. There are no victims!

If you choose to view your life through the lens of personal power, then no matter the circumstances, outside influences, outcome, or trivial details your ego can conjure up, you will experience yourself as having been powerful in that situation.

Here's where the magic comes in: like any belief, personal power functions as a muscle: The more you work it, the stronger it gets. This means that as you exercise your personal power, execute choices that reinforce your invincibility, and trust your ability to make decisions congruent with your life purpose, your personal power will exponentially grow.

If, on the other hand, you pick up the lens of personal disempowerment, failure, and screw-up, every single thing you do and result you achieve (or don't achieve) may be diminished or disregarded because you have chosen to represent yourself as a train wreck. And guess what? Everyone you encounter may then see you that way; because you will emit a vibe that says, "I am a major mess. Caution, I am contagious."

Initiate Impact!

1. What is an example of one time when you took a challenging situation and found success (whatever your definition of that is)?
   ◆ Re-write the event through the lens of a victim.
   ◆ Now re-write the event through the lens of personal power.

2. What is the difference between the two stories?
3. How can you apply this learning to a current situation in your professional or personal life?
4. Did you view Janine as a victim or hero?
   ◆ Why?
5. Think of a situation in your life that makes you feel out of control.
   ◆ What can you do to gain control in the situation?

Essay 10

The Man Is the Head, But the Woman Is the Neck!

Masculine and Feminine Power

The term *personal power* is probably one of the most overused, least understood, and improperly applied terms in our lexicon. Why? The way we define, apply, and interact with one another's personal power is in a state of flux in response to the transition occurring in our global community. Power is the currency used to evaluate these transitions.

When we used to think about personal power, what usually came to mind was one person having power over another. For instance, The Golden Rule: "He who makes the gold makes the rules." Although I'm not insinuating that you or I agree with this cultural paradigm, it is, nevertheless, an accurate representation. As women this has meant *patriarchal traditions* having "power over" us. It was born of the ego, the intellect, and the material and represented the objective, rational, and political.

This masculine form of power is antithetical to just about everything associated with women, including our biological makeup and how we've been socialized. Feminine personal power is "power with" and it excludes one-upmanship, and "power over."

> Personal Power is the measure of our ability to access the internal and external resources that support our best and highest good.

Fancy schmancy definition aside, if the answer is personal power, then the question is, *"Can you get what you want or what you need if it will be in your best interest to do so?"*

Personal power may appear to be a complex and monumental concept. It is easy to recognize in others, although difficult to see in our self. It is particularly ambiguous for women: While we are fast in recognizing when we're disempowering ourselves, we can have a blind spot for those times when we're standing firmly in our power and asserting ourselves. We sometimes just don't *allow* ourselves to see how great we are!

To illustrate: Have you ever noticed how easy it is to acknowledge and take ownership of a mistake you've made, but how uncomfortable it is to take equal measure of credit when you've excelled? How often every day do you throw out "I'm sorry"? But how quickly do you brush off thanks and gratitude from another? That would be the point!

We experience a sense of power when we feel in control of our lives: when we're healthy, earning a plentiful income, in loving relationships, working in a career that satisfies us. Success and happiness are purportedly ushered in by personal power. We're taught that it helps us to achieve our goals, influence others, communicate effectively, master our destiny, and hold sway over our environment. These things are masculine forms of power inasmuch as they are something we 'get' or 'do' in the physical world.

That, however, is the smaller part of the formula. Power on the physical level is vulnerable to people and circumstances beyond our controllable dominion. The minute our world changes for reasons beyond our influence, this type of personal power can vaporize as well. Our job can go away, the economy can go bust, our relationship can walk out the door, and the money can run out, whatever. It's called living from the outside in, and it's a date with disaster.

Living within that masculine model makes us susceptible to giving our power exclusively to factors beyond the very control
we sought.

The sheer beauty and ease of living in/from a feminine paradigm is
that it's internal; it's our connectedness with our Self and God and that
relationship is sacred and pure. As you deepen your engagement with
your God Self, as you become more and more intimate with the deepest
levels of your emotional and spiritual bodies, you come to realize that
as long as you have your Self, you can be safe and at peace. While an
infinite number of factors can change the way your life looks, without
your consent, there is nothing or no one who can impact your internal
sense of well being without your permission.

■ ■ ■

A few years ago I coached a gentleman who had inherited tens of
millions of dollars. In his late thirties he was, by self-admission, utterly
without purpose. He had the funds to do whatever he wanted with his
life, and still suffered from acute anxiety and depression. The primary
reason he was so unhappy is that he did not earn that money on his
own; he never got to see what he was capable of creating, he never
got to strut his stuff. As humans, we have an urge to discover how far
we can take ourselves. When we are never pushed to our limits, we
become desperate in our efforts to prove ourselves in other ways.

This masculine model of *power over* continues to fail to produce
the results it promises. Right now, as you sit reading these words in the
relative comfort of your life, there are 143 million orphans in the world,
12.5 percent of the American population (37.3 million people) is living
in poverty, and 37.4 million people in the world are living as refugees.
I wouldn't call that a system that is working, would you?

Which brings us back to the matter of transition. The proverbial
pendulum is swaying in the other direction—toward a feminine framework.

However, let's not do a happy dance just yet: While we're in the process of distancing ourselves *from* this masculine model, we are not yet racing *toward* the feminine one.

We actually need some aspects of both. In the hilarious movie, *My Big Fat Greek Wedding,* the "girls" point out that while "the man is the head, the woman is the neck." This, of course, means that although the man thinks he is in charge of the family, the woman steers him in the direction she wants him to go; leaving us knowing who is *really* in charge.

We're increasingly ready for the feminine qualities that have been so undervalued in our culture. We need the mutually enhancing power that characterizes feminine relationships. We need the harmony and balance that are the glue of the feminine model. We are collectively exhausted by over thinking everything, hiding in our heads, and excluding our now crucial need to access the feminine energy we already possess. By frequently subordinating our need for nurturance, by perpetuating the patterns that distance us from our purpose, we have evolved into a neurotic, unfulfilled, and imbalanced culture. We don't really want to continue this way, do we?

At the same time that we're in real need of heart-centered activity, we also need the structure, the solid container that the masculine provides. This is an *and* conversation, not an either/or. Once the feminine, the heart, has felt something, intuited it (whatever 'it' may be), then we need that masculine part of us to go out and get it done; in tandem. A team. The feminine feels it; the masculine part of us carries out the order; the head and the neck.

Here's a concrete example: Your inner voice, your intuition tells you, "It's time to find a new home!" Of course you question that voice several times because there is no way that voice is accurate: Your landlord just renewed your lease; you're settled in with your family. Sure enough, two weeks after you receive this incoming message from your intuition, your landlord advises you that the house you're living in is about to be repossessed. You were right after all! You scurry to find a new home. The feminine got the message. The masculine fulfills the message by looking for a new house.

Just as only 10 percent of an iceberg appears above water, if there were a device to measure personal power, we would find that only 10 percent of our personal power is visible in concrete terms. This is the masculine measure of our power. The 90 percent balance is unseen and lives within the individual. That is the feminine.

Being cerebral is a great attribute; so long as you have the feminine included in your life's picture as well. Being emotional, sensitive, and heart-centered is an easy way to live; so long as you have the masculine within you to keep you grounded. We need both parts of ourselves collaborating for a common purpose: That purpose is personal power.

To the extent that we are personally powerful and that we own that power, we are able to access every molecule of personal strength, integrity, courage, trust, faith, honor, and so on, at will and on demand. Internal resources are represented by non-tangibles, by what is often referred to as a person's character. While we may see evidence of our internal resources, we can't visually see the resources themselves. Personal Power also means that we're able to access the external resources that will support our best and highest good. This is the physical aspect of power—the things we can actually see, that result from the cultivation of our internal power.

This transition we're in may not be an easy one. The masculine model of leadership is the only one we've known for hundreds of years. We don't like the new way of doing things because we have to make it up as we go along, which means we have to trust ourselves. Trusting ourselves challenges us to challenge our beliefs. Challenging our beliefs can lead to upset. The whole thing can be quite confusing and uncomfortable.

Note: The dynamic between your internal masculine (the part of you that accomplishes tasks) and your internal feminine (the part of you that senses emotions and intuits what needs to be accomplished) is an *exact* replica of your relationship with your significant other. Now that's something to think about!

Initiate Impact!

1. Where in your life are you feeling powerful right now?
2. Where in your life are you feeling short on power?
3. How do these things impact your ability to function highly at work? At home?
4. What would need to happen, today, for you to get in balance?
5. What do you perceive is standing in your way and keeping that from happening?

Part Three

What Undermines Impact?

Essay 11

If You Don't Know Where You're Going, How Will You Know When You Arrive?

Meandering through Life

Me: "What do you want?"

Her: "What do you mean?"

Me: "What do you want?"

Her: "Huh?" (Confusion spreading like wildfire all over her face.)

Me: "What do you want?"

Her: "I don't understand the question." (Uncensored panic replaces said confusion.)

Me: "Okay, I'll ask you another way—what do you want?" (Giggles in the background.)

Her: "I just don't understand what you mean!" (Frustration now flooding her face.)

Me: "Yeah, I get that."

Laughter comes from behind me, and irritability from in front of me.

Let me give you some background. It's Saturday morning, and the second day of a three-day training I facilitate. It's called *Women. Courage. Leadership.*™ for a reason. We're on location for one of my favorite clients, whose name is synonymous with software. Thirty-five of the sharpest women I've ever had the privilege to work with are seated, horseshoe style, pens and pads in hand anxiously anticipating what will happen next. That legendary pin could have dropped; so taut was the tension in that room that I turned to the group and reminded them to breathe.

To create perspective, it is important to know that these women were meticulously selected to attend this retreat based on a number of rigorous criteria, including their professional level, their proximity to high potential status, and the recommendation of their managers. Attendance was voluntary; and, like everything else in this high-status organization, the competition was staggering.

When the invitation to the retreat was e-mailed to 480 women in this organization, every spot was filled within 27 minutes. Within 45 minutes, another 180 women were wait-listed. I'd like to think that their reaction was in response to my reputation and the results my work produces. But truthfully, I think it had more to do with the yearning factor—these high-tech women were starving for some low-tech attention to their feminine side.

> They were betting three days of their lives that the course would offer them an opportunity to amp up their personal power, find their life's purpose, and pursue a bit of passion.

They wanted to find their own way, stand in their authentic selves, and walk with dignity and grace.

But back to the group scenario: I stood in front of these women thinking to myself, "Houston, we have a problem." This was not *at all* how I'd planned this segment of the program. We were "supposed" to be concentrating on what was in the way of their getting what they wanted; not starting from ground zero, merely figuring out what that might be. Eighteen years of doing these kinds of trainings, however, made me more flexible than Gumby. So I put aside my own agenda and picked up theirs.

I turned toward the woman in the hot seat and inquired, "What do you want your life to look like? How do you want it to feel? What are your dreams?" This wonderfully successful, multitalented, high-IQ woman finally understood my question. Forlornly—her shoulders slumped, her eyes welling a bit—she said, "I don't know. I don't know what I want."

"How is it that you don't know what you want?" I quietly asked her while, to be candid, the speech bubble over my head read: "You are 36 years old. How did you get here without knowing what you wanted?" Compassion; concern; confusion. Those were my feelings, not hers.

I looked up to see 34 women holding their breath, frozen looks on most of their faces. The speech bubble over those heads read: "Please, dear God, don't let Nancy call on me next."

I went around the room asking others the same question, "What do you want?" Face after face repeated, "I don't know." Some were embarrassed, some angry, some bewildered; no one was neutral. Periodically, one of the women would tell me precisely what she had in mind for herself. Those are the moments in which I exhaled.

You may be thinking to yourself, "Do you seriously believe that these women didn't *know* what they wanted?" While they certainly had, at some point in their lives, asked themselves these questions, it had been quite some time, based on their responses, the looks on their faces, and feel of the room. It was obvious to me that the majority of these women weren't creating their lives; they were chasing them.

Of course, it's possible that they simply didn't want to share their intimate thoughts with their peers; that as much as they liked one another, if push came to shove, these women were still competitors. Perhaps they were concerned that confidentiality would be broken, or that one woman would hold another woman's feelings hostage. But I don't think so. The emotional climate in that room said more than I could hope to explain. You really had to be there.

Can you and I agree that if you don't know what you want, your chances of getting it are right up there with the lottery and lightning?

As I discuss in this Essay, if you don't know where you're going, how will you know when you arrive? And that's exactly where most of these women ended up.

The question "Why don't you know what you want?" is subordinate to the question, "What do you want?" (no judgment, no shame), just as "What do you want for dinner?" is ancillary to "Are you hungry?" Like the rest of life, change began with asking the right questions.

Disregarding the clock, I then circled the room with a singular query: "Why do you think that you don't know what you want?" As though they had all ordered from the same very limited menu, two answers came back to me:

- ◆ "No one has ever asked me that question before."
- ◆ "I've never asked myself that question."

I am not making this up.

It was my turn to be shocked into silence; and, let me tell you, I am seldom without words. The question dangling before me was this: Had something happened to these women on their way up the corporate ladder (or, for that matter, in the culture); or had something critical failed to happen? I suspected it was both.

My head was swirling with questions. Could it be true that these women actually lacked a vision for their lives? Or would it be more accurate to say that their vision had been shut down and locked away?

- ◆ Had it been taken from them?
- ◆ Did they have a vision that they just couldn't get to?
- ◆ Had someone or something argued them out of their dreams, so their hopes retreated into obscurity?
- ◆ Had their vision simply atrophied from lack of exercise, or had they never even had one?

And what did this disconnect imply? What were the ramifications of having a sizable cohort disengaged from the question, "*What did I come here to do and am I getting it done?*"

I planted myself solidly in the middle of the room, while the women waited for the leader (that would be me) to do something, anything, to fix this mystifying and inconvenient problem called "Super Software Company has a population of highly talented women who don't know what they want to do with their lives." (It did occur to me at the time that maybe this particular group deliberately signed up for the retreat because they knew they didn't know what they should know.) What was particularly confounding is that this company has the reputation of being a veritable laboratory of innovation, a Petri dish for creativity.

- ◆ Why would these women have given more thought to promoting their business than to supporting themselves?
- ◆ Why would they have attended more to the wardrobe on their backs than to the value of their values?
- ◆ Why did they spend more time on their dinner plans than on their life plans?

At that point, there were lots of questions with very few answers. Super Software Company had initially brought me in for the sole purpose of determining why its female talent was leaving the organization immediately prior to promotions into leadership roles.

> The company was investing heavily in its latent talent who, just when they were about to reach their objectives, were self-selecting out of the game.

Super Software Company was throwing untold revenue, time, and energy down a black hole. It wanted to know why these women were migrating elsewhere, and what they could do about it.

I decided to set aside the retreat handbook in favor of exploring why these women seemed to be meandering through their lives and, if that were so, what they could do about it.

Round and round we went all afternoon, venting, exploring, discovering, creating, and then making it up when we didn't know what we were doing. I dedicated the day to helping them sort through the cultural debris of their lives so they might find the pieces of themselves they'd lost or misplaced.

What did I learn? That beneath the rhetoric that said otherwise—behind the confidence and the bravado—these women were like every other woman I'd ever worked with. They did, indeed, have a vision; and they did, indeed, have a dream. They had made a promise to themselves, a contract that had yet to expire. All these things were laying dormant, waiting for them to get the confidence, the self-permission, and the loving support and guidance that would allow them to remember what they were built for. They just needed an environment that would embrace and support all of who they were. They needed to give themselves permission to be more than their next project, bigger than next year's promotion, and greater than the person they'd been pretending to be.

I labeled the day "Mission Possible!" And it was!

As the retreat concluded, I wondered if the women at Super Software Company were an anomaly. Were they an isolated case, or was such absence of self-awareness widespread (if unspoken of) in corporate America? I surmised that because women represented less than 20 percent of the population of this company, there might be something in their corporate culture that precluded them from meaningfully engaging themselves at a core level. This possibility was further bolstered by the knowledge that a certain type of woman, with a proclivity toward the masculine end of the energy spectrum, and with a skill set stereotypically (although not necessarily accurately) attributed to men, is drawn to the high-tech industry. (Ladies, do not get your thong in a knot over this statement. Central tendencies merely indicate that this statement is true more often than it is not; and, of course, this assumption does not necessarily apply to you or anyone you know.)

After the retreat, I went about the business of my business, traveling to various parts of the country, and conducting my own little nonscientific, ad hoc study on women and self-engagement. Within a few months the irrefutable evidence was in:

> Women who don't know what they want (or, if they do, how to get it) can be found in every nook and cranny of this country.

I discovered that, frequently, if they do know what they want, then it is a "thing"—like a relationship or a house or a relationship or a promotion or a car or a man or a relationship. (You're not alone: The confirmation of that stereotype pissed me off, too!) This is not to imply that there aren't any women anywhere who know what they want; it's merely to suggest that there are far too many women who are (unnecessarily) rudderless in their lives.

Everywhere I traveled, whether for business or socially, I'd ask women the question, "What do you want?" Everywhere I went, the answers remained virtually the same. "I don't know" was interspersed with "I don't know how to get it," "I wish I could...," "I'm hoping that...," "If only...." OMG.

Initiate Impact!

1. How does not knowing what you want impact your life choices?
2. What do you want for your life personally?
   a. Professionally?
   b. In the next year, 5 years, 10 years?
3. How do you think knowing what you want impacts your organization? Your family?
4. Had you attended this retreat, what two questions might you have asked these women?

Essay 12

The Hidden 'I' in Invisible

Life Unnoticed

Colleen: I walked into the car dealership ready to buy. I brought my husband along, so he could pick the color and kick the tires. The salesman looked past me as though I were invisible. He headed straight for my husband, assuming that *he* was the one buying the car. I walked out with my checkbook.

Sue: I'm the only woman in our engineering company. I was in a management meeting with eight of my colleagues. Ten minutes in, we were trying to figure out a solution to a costly, long-term problem. I knew immediately what we had to do. I made my argument for why we needed to implement X, Y, and Z. Nobody seemed to hear me, and they moved on. An hour later, I reintroduced the same solution; I packaged it without the passion and presented only the data, thinking it would be easier for the team to hear. No go. Three hours later, Parker regurgitated my idea as his own, and the crowd went wild. Inside, so did I. That was *my* genius idea! I felt as though I didn't even exist. Had I raised my voice to be heard, they would have told me I was too emotional. They have no idea how happy they should have been that I wasn't armed!

Vicki: For 5 years I told my husband that I wasn't happy with our sex life: Being intimate once every two weeks just wasn't

72

enough for me. Every week, we had the same conversation. He told me I was oversexed; I told him twice-weekly sex did not qualify me as a candidate for sex addiction rehab. After five years, I headed for the door. You should have seen his face! He was shocked—like this was the very first time he had heard that I needed more physical contact. Clueless! He told me I was being difficult, hysterical, hard to manage, too demanding. I can't let you print what I told him in response.

(Your Story) _____

_____

_____

_____

_____

_____

■ ■ ■

Invisible.

Any elaboration is superfluous. Ask any woman about it; in fact, ask *every* woman about it. She'll exuberantly shake her head in your direction, signaling her concern, her compassion, and her condolences. At this point in her life, she has confronted it so many times and so consistently that she has accepted it, become exhausted by it, or is fighting it with every sliver of self-respect she can garner. Surrender? Never! Some of us would rather eat broken glass in a department store window—naked.

> There are two kinds of invisible. The kind we *agree* to, and the kind we *initiate*. Both render us powerless and diminish our impact.

The distinction is so subtle, so imperceptible, that most women aren't even aware that there is one. And even if they are conscious of this difference, they may be blind to the fact that they have a choice—they can either perpetuate or dismantle the *invisibility myth*. We don't seem to realize that we have a say in the matter, or even that there is a matter in which to *have* a say. When we are raised in a home with a wood-burning stove, we become immune to the smell of smoke. When we are raised in a society that renders women invisible, it takes a strong disruption in our life to notice this, and to realize that there is an alternative. We always have choices, not always with regard to what happens in life, but always with regard to what we think about it and what our attitude will be about it.

■ ■ ■

"Invisible" by Agreement: Acceptance, Consent, Acquiescence, Endorsement

It's overt. It's conspicuous. Some person, group, or organization says or does something that influences or impacts us in such a way to render invisibility. And what do we women do? Nothing. We take what we're given; that's it. We forget that when we say nothing about an injustice, it still casts a vote—although a silent one. The difference here is merely technical. We inadvertently agree with a culture that subordinates us—that treats us as "not as good as," "less than," or "other"—when these kinds of things occur and we choose to do nothing about it.

> When we say and/or do nothing in defense of our values, principles, gender, and selves—and instead tolerate the exploitation—we are, in essence, agreeing with and accepting the status quo.

Then we quietly consent to our delegated and diluted role by playing it small, keeping quiet, and censoring what we say. And when we relinquish our power, we pass that same torch on to the generations of women who will follow us—the women for whom we are supposed to act as role models.

1. *We choose to accept inequitable pay in our jobs.*
   - We don't want anyone to think we're troublemakers; and hey, at least we *have* a job.
2. *Someone else's name is on our slide deck during the national sales conference and we choose not to bring it up.*
   - It would be so trivial; after all, it was a *team* effort.
3. *A relative decides to use us for target practice at Thanksgiving dinner.*
   - We say nothing to our parents. Despite the gravy she dumped on your head, it's really no big deal, because your relative has "issues."
4. *We're passed over for a well-deserved promotion.*
   - We don't say anything because the guy who got it has three kids.
5. *We stay in an abusive relationship.*
   - He only emotionally abuses us when he's been drinking, on national holidays and on alternate Thursdays. Oh, and when his mother calls. Besides, what will he do without us?
6. *We don't argue when confronted with a problem we had nothing to do with—we just roll over.*
   - Confrontation is so unpleasant: It will make us look like we're not a team player, we're a bitch, or we're a bitch who's not a team player.
7. _____
   _____
   _____
   _____

■ ■ ■

INITIATE INVISIBLE: COMMENCE, INSTIGATE, LAUNCH

Some women do or say nothing to advance themselves or get what they want. They lay claim to nothing; they demand nothing. It's an absence of activity on their own behalf, which contrasts with *agreeing* to invisibility by merely tolerating it (although there can certainly be overlap between the initiation and the agreement of our invisibility).

While agreeing to invisibility is a lack of response to something someone else does, initiating invisibility is a lack of response or direct action on our own behalf.

It's one thing when someone ignores you in a meeting; it's another when you ignore yourself.

When we initiate our invisibility, we do so in response to a core belief that we're not worthy of "it"; we don't deserve it; we're not lovable so we can't have it, or we're not _____ enough (smart enough, educated enough, pretty enough, and the like). These core beliefs are explained, in detail, in Essay #25. We choose to render ourselves unworthy of even taking up space, and feel that we should pay a surcharge on the air we breathe. We neither volunteer our voice in protest, nor vocalize our preferences. We wear schmaltzy tee shirts that say, "Doormat," and we actually think they're funny. We see something we want and we do nothing to get it.

1. *We don't ask for what we want.*
   - That would be selfish.
2. *We do nothing to get recognition at our company.*
   - We don't want to appear egocentric, too big for our britches, or as though we're vying for a promotion (which we happen to be doing).
3. *We don't vote: It's only one little vote, anyway.*
   - Reminder: Not voting is voting, too. (No vote. No voice. No choice.)
4. *We don't speak up in a brainstorming meeting when we have brilliant ideas to contribute.*
   - We don't want to appear to be not bright, and the exposure means so much more to Ann Marie.
5. *We fail to throw our hats in the ring when a promotion comes up.*
   - Phil needs it more than we do.
6. *We're asked to present a case for the budget we need for the new project.*

- We relinquish the dollars instead of presenting the case, because we're not very good at coming up with a rational argument for what we know, in our bones, is a solid case.
7. *We volunteer to hand over our share of the family's discretionary funds.*
   - Instead of taking that spa vacation with our college friends, we let our husband buy a new fishing rod. After all, we just went to the spa 12 years ago before our four children were born, and he works so hard every day as a supervisor at his company.

_____

_____

_____

■ ■ ■

Which 'I' in invisible are you?

Are you the I who, albeit unintentionally, consents to women's invisibility? Are you the I who initiates your own invisibility? Most of us have found ourselves in both of these arenas at one time or another. On rare occasions, I've found myself stopping midstride, having just observed that I'd had a momentary lapse of reason; and there I was, again, in the victim position, forfeiting a choice I hadn't even realized I had.

Perhaps you learned by example that being visible was dangerous, scary, a threat? Perhaps it made you too accountable, responsible, vulnerable, or powerful? Perhaps it's something you want to change? Women don't set out to encourage invisibility. It's systemic. It's pervasive. It's inevitable. And until someone points it out to us, most of us hardly notice it; or, if we do, we just take it for granted that it's right up there with death and taxes. Check as many as you'd like:

☐ Do you deserve to be honored?
☐ Do you deserve respect?

☐ Are your contributions worthy of being heard?
☐ Do you have substance?
☐ Do you have grace?
☐ Do you have wisdom?
☐ Do you bring value to the world?
☐ Do you deserve to be loved?

Why ask these questions? Because it's important that you respond yes to all of them so that others will too. We can only be seen if we first see ourselves. We can only be heard if we're willing to hear ourselves. We can only have impact if we deem that we are valuable. And it's a choice. Like everything else, we get to decide who 'I' will be in my world. Not choosing means someone else will choose for us. That's not okay with you, is it?

Initiate Impact!

1. How do you assure your visibility at work?
2. What did you learn about being an invisible woman that interferes with what you want to accomplish today?
3. If you were to be visible in every aspect of your life, who would you need to be and what would you need to do?

Essay 13

That's Not a Doormat, It's My Back!

Selfish, Selfirst, Selfless

> How many Jewish grandmothers does it take to change a lightbulb?
>
> None. "Don't worry about me. I'll just sit here in the dark and go blind."

My mother, in labor with me, delayed her trip to the hospital so that she could make my father scrambled eggs for breakfast. I am *not* kidding. She gave birth to me two hours later. She laughs bitterly when she tells this story and exclaims, "That man was so selfish that on the day you were born. . . ." My question is this: Was he *selfish* or was she *selfless*?

From the stance of "there are no victims," my mother had a choice to make the moment her husband asked for breakfast. Honestly, that moment came years before when she first accepted this type of behavior from him. Is either of them at fault? No! They are merely accountable for a dynamic they both signed on for.

For thousands of years we have been socialized to subjugate and suppress our needs in deference to, well, just about everyone else. Just as this country's soil no longer contains the nutrients necessary to keep us healthy because we have overused it, we women have been maxed out in the giving department with scarce opportunity for self-rejuvenation.

Somewhere along the road, many women are taught that to put themselves at the top of their own priority list is selfish, egocentric, self-absorbed, inconsiderate, uncaring, and incongruent with what it stereotypically means to be a woman. Unfortunately, these women have grown to agree with that conclusion, and perpetuate that myth with self-neglect. I won't bore you with the oxygen mask metaphor, but most of us need to be occasionally reminded that the world is only as healthy, and society only as educated, as its women: Disconnected and disengaged women breed more of the same.

■ ■ ■

> Self-neglect has, in recent years, earned a cult-like reputation.

There are some fundamental distinctions that need to be made between women who are *selfish* and those who are *selfless*. In Essay #25 we explore the topic of core wounds, and how they insidiously rule our lives when unexposed and unhealed. Selfish and selfless essentially sprout from the same core wound: *I'm not enough.*

Selfish people are those who are primarily concerned with their own wants and needs, and don't take anyone else's into consideration. It truly is all about them all the time. Why? At their core, these people feel as though they are not enough, so there will never be enough of anything to fill the hole or void within them. Anything that comes within their reach, whether it's time, attention, things, money, you name it, are held onto in desperation. When people are selfish, their mentality is focused on lack and scarcity—the world is not enough because they are not enough. This concept is further elaborated on in Essay #13 where we explore our outside physical world as a three-dimensional expression of how we feel about ourselves.

As I mentioned previously, the selfless woman also has the "I'm not enough" core wound. She believes she is so lacking, so deficient as a human being that if she isn't constantly making herself valuable and useful by doing for others, then no one would keep her around. We all know women who trip over themselves to do something for us and, predictably, they usually go overboard. It may be the mother who offers to carpool both ways every day for a month, with no expectations that you will reciprocate. It may be the office "mom" who brings in baked goods three days a week, and always remembers your favorites. It could be the mother who allows her children and spouse to take and take and take and take, as she continues to give and give and give and give, with no bottom in sight. This woman, at an unconscious level, believes that if she stops doing nice things for everyone, no one would want to know her; no one would see that she has any value as a human being, because she finds no value in herself.

Lastly, there is our best friend, "Selfull," aka "Selfirst." These are women who are healthy, happy, and well-adjusted, most of the time. Most of the time? A person does not exist who, on occasion, does not slip into selfless or selfish mode. It is the contrast that is necessary to keep us powerful. Ms. Selfirst makes sure that she's eaten breakfast because she has a very full day in front of her and she knows that if she's not on top of her game, she could end up at the bottom of the heap—no vehicle can run without sufficient fuel. Ms. Selfirst has pretty healthy boundaries; she has a good sense of what works for her and what doesn't. Sometimes she will alter her own boundaries, and she is aware of when she does it and why she does it.

Ms. Selfirst is uncomfortable telling someone "No" when that person needs her, but she's willing to do it just the same. She has such self-esteem that she allows herself to "break the rules" on a whim. Perhaps she was once a doormat, but she came to realize what motivated her to give inappropriately. She felt awful about having been so needy and equally bad about everyone who took advantage of her. Rather than bring her close to these people, acting this way distanced her because she didn't respect herself and no one else did, either. She raised her self-worth, she grew to realize that she was "enough," and now she is surrounded by people who share her healthy opinion of herself.

■ ■ ■

There is a world of difference between an individual having needs and an individual being needy. Everyone has needs—spiritual, emotional, mental, and physical. This is healthy and normal, and is not only to be expected but is desirable, as well. We live much longer when we recognize and take care of our needs.

The category of "needy" is an entirely different game, and not the healthy one we want to aspire to play. When people are needy they are co-dependent, clingy, outwardly focused, and lacking the emotional infrastructure to take care of their own needs. A needy individual may not feel she is capable of taking care of herself, so she looks to others to do that for her. You will identify her as an energy sucker—simply being in her presence exhausts and drains you.

The selfish and selfless are known more for their negative impact than for anything else.

> There is no room for *you* in a relationship with a selfish person because he or she takes up all the space. There is too much room in a relationship with a selfless person because he or she takes up no space at all.

In both of these relationships you will either feel very lonely or you will resort to caretaking behavior yourself. It is the selfirst woman who is on purpose in her life, is personally powerful, and has the most positive impact.

The women who are selfish or selfless may not necessarily be the superstars in the office. Their hidden agendas are anything but hidden. Colleagues sense that these women are inauthentic and lost. They feel manipulated by these women's behavior and are aware that it is aimed at the woman feeling good about herself and not about the generosity of giving. They know that her gestures and kindnesses have nothing to do with a genuine desire to assist and support them.

Whether you have a tendency to be that selfless doormat or that selfish, self-centered egotist is not nearly as significant as what you do with that learning. Few people are completely in selfirst all of the time. Our primary responsibility to ourselves is to know in which direction we lean when we're stressed, and to accommodate for that in our lives.

Initiate Impact!

1. What circumstances in your life bring out the selfless woman in you?
   - What do you notice about that tendency in you?
2. What circumstances in your life bring out the selfish woman in you?
   - What do you notice about that tendency in you?
3. What circumstances in your life bring out the selfirst woman in you?
   - What do you notice about that tendency in you?

Don't Take the Last Piece of Pie
Putting Yourself Last

A man enters a room with one thing on his mind—food. As he passes through, he turns to his friends and family and says, "I'm hungry. I'm going to get something to eat." End of story.

A woman walks into the same room. It's 5:00 in the evening. As usual, she has been insanely busy and has forgotten to eat all day. Since she woke at 6:00 this morning, she has done three loads of laundry, gone to the grocery store, picked up the dry cleaning, dropped off each of her three children at their various activities, gone into the office, responded to 470 e-mails, and essentially solved every problem that came her way except for world peace. She is starving. Her stomach is growling. She's a bit cranky and faint. She says, "Is anybody hungry?"

He's hungry. He gets something to eat. She's hungry; she offers to feed everybody else. Why do we do that? It's not just a matter of manners; it goes much deeper than that. No news flash here: Women have been socialized to be "other" centered, and our physiology conveniently reinforces that fact. We've been taught to be caretaker, caregiver, care for, care—period.

Nowhere does it say or is it written that we should take care of others, but grossly neglect, ignore, and deny our own needs. *That* we learned on our own.

Many years ago, when I was in the process of adopting my daughter, I had a conversation with my mother that succinctly characterizes the struggle that many women face today in attempting to have their needs met.

Me:　I've been interviewing nannies all afternoon.
Mom: What do you need a nanny for?
Me:　Well, you know, when I want to get out of the house, go to the gym, get my nails done, take care of myself....
Mom: You're a mother now. *You don't get to have any needs!*

There's a joke in there somewhere; but I've yet to find it.

■ ■ ■

Sociologically, women are still the keepers of the nest and the minder of the relationships. As much as we've advanced in traditional male industries such as technology, medicine, quantum physics, and the like, the one thing that has endured over time is the role of women in the family. While our presence in the workforce has dramatically changed, our responsibilities at home have barely inched forward; our domestic duties are astonishingly similar to what they were 50 years ago. By securing employment outside the home, much of what we have done is to merely add a full-time job to the one we already had—except this one comes with a paycheck.

Our self-esteem is tethered to the quality of our relationships, both personally and professionally. Nowhere is this truer than in our relationships with our family members—they need us and we need to be needed. As relationship-centered beings, we unceasingly herd those around us. We check to see how our friends are doing; we mother the younger generations with whom we work; we take the emotional temperature of any random group in which we happen to find ourselves; and we befriend women who do the same. As much as the adage is that "when Mom's happy, everyone's happy," what is equally accurate is that "when everyone's happy, Mom's especially happy—she's done her job well!"

It has been recurrently drilled into most females that it is selfish to take care of our needs before others'. From an early age, most of us have been taught *not* to display our power. We are encouraged to fit in, avoid making waves, accommodate others' desires above our own, be modest in our self-appraisal, and keep a lid on our ego. And it is *never* okay to take care of our needs before someone else's at the risk of appearing un-nurturing, unfeminine, and selfish. The tendency to avoid calling attention to ourselves—to dim the lights on our own brilliance and deflect positive attention—is a major factor in our invisibility. Making the conscious choice to change those things in ourselves will catapult us into our invincibility.

■ ■ ■

> The biggest challenge women have when entertaining the notion of leadership is that it seems to conflict with our relationship model: *"You can't be part of the group you're trying to lead."*

In order to be effective leaders, we have to literally step out of the group and go solo. Consequently, *we* become "other": which unwittingly can make us betrayer, full of ourselves, conceited, braggart, and so on. Becoming a leader often forces us to bump up against the female cultural paradigm of collaboration and inclusion; something that in the women's club is tantamount to treason.

Oh, and did I mention that we should never show the guys how smart we are? Do you know that some women are still teaching their daughters this nonsense?

In my line of work, I repeatedly find myself in front of women who are angry, frustrated, or resigned because they are not getting the recognition they deserve at work; and are, subsequently, overlooked for promotions.

> In fact, lack of recognition is one of the primary reasons that women are leaving corporate America at twice the rate of men.

At the office and at home, it is assumed to be our responsibility to take care of others; to supply recognition to those around us, and to relinquish our own need to be seen. We've been conditioned to think that to take recognition for oneself is to deny it to others—which for most of us is as impossible as taking the last piece of pie or spending the last dollar on ourselves. We live in fear that getting recognition or praise will come at someone else's expense and, unfortunately, too many of us would prefer to pass up an opportunity rather than be labeled as self-absorbed.

Add to this mix years of training in which we were taught not to stand out, stand up, and be outstanding. Demanding attention for ourselves also breaks the rules of other-centeredness. We incorrectly assume that attention to ourselves denies someone else attention—as though there's a finite quantity of attention to go around. If you think about it, it's really a scarcity mentality, a mindset of "lack."

Here's the conundrum: How will anyone know we did a great job if we're unwilling or unable to share the very information that will lead them to that conclusion? How do we express our ambition, announce our accomplishments, and reap the rewards that recognition brings while staying true to and celebrating our femininity?

The answer? Very carefully, consciously, and powerfully.

We have the propensity to sacrifice our own feelings, desires, and ambitions so that others won't feel bad. Think about how dumb this truly is. Why are *our* feelings less valuable than someone else's? Is it martyrdom? It's like saying that while *we* can take disappointment, rejection, unintended outcomes—our mother, friend, colleague, neighbor, or partner can't. This is actually quite arrogant of us. If there's one life vest left and the ship is going down, the healthy people will lay claim to that vest. It's called the desire to live.

■ ■ ■

Not long ago, a colleague attended one of my weekend retreats. At its conclusion, she told me that while the information was life altering for her, what *really* blew her away was her experience of my huge heart and my capacity to empathize—*especially* given my reputation as being extremely ambitious, a real go-getter. Ouch!

I was stunned by both her candor and its content. I cringe to think that this fellow professional couldn't (or wouldn't) place my capacity to emotionally engage in the same equation as my ambition to achieve. Like most of our culture, she is of the opinion that to have ambition in the form of fame, fortune, or position is absolutely incongruent with what it means to be feminine and relationally oriented.

Did she mean that I had to choose? I could be either feminine or ambitious, and I couldn't be both; or at least, not at the same time? And as for my so-called reputation—I truly believe we earn those and that we're in charge of them; so if I seem very ambitious, it's because I'm, well, very ambitious. I set the bar very high because I have so much to do before my life is done. I've never, even for a moment, suspended my femininity in my quest for success. As a matter of fact, I'd attribute my success largely to my femininity. It's most likely that this colleague wasn't even conscious of what she said. That's how it is with cultural tendencies; they're so much a part of who we are that we don't even notice them. And that is what makes them so dangerous, to begin with.

The question of whether ambition is acceptable in women has already been answered. The next generation question is, "What do we do about it?" How do we perform at our potential, exceed our own expectations, *and* celebrate our femininity?

When it's distilled down, this is a conversation about women, our personal power and our relationship to ourselves. When we are uncomfortable with and afraid of our own power, we would rather sacrifice it to those around us than learn how to take responsibility for it. I suspect that we fear discovering that when we display our stuff, no one will want to play with us—that we'll alienate the very people we've worked so diligently at getting to know.

Contemplate this: There is not one thing noble about playing small, diminutive, and insignificant. There's not one thing enviable about feeding our families and not ourselves. There has never been a more perfect time for us to rethink our job as role models for the next generations of women and girls. What *do* we want our impact to be, as women, mothers, daughters, executives, homemakers, and professionals? To the future female role models, do we want to bequeath scarcity, fear, invisibility, disempowerment, and neediness? *Or* impact, invincibility, courage, and leadership?

What is so exhilarating about this time in history is that we are one of the first generations of women to consciously choose our legacy, just as we are deliberately choosing our impact. In order to carry out that obligation with integrity, however, we must live the legacy first. Are *you* up for the challenge?

Initiate Impact!

1. In what areas of your life do you most neglect yourself?
    *   Why is your self-neglect in those areas?
2. If you were to take care of yourself as you might your best friend, what would you do?
    *   When will you begin to do it?
    *   How can you make yourself accountable for this plan?
3. What do you need to change in order to stand up and be out-standing in your life?
    *   What could you accomplish professionally as the result of mak-ing that change?
4. In order to put yourself at the top of your priority list, you would need to establish some new boundaries in your relationships. List three in order of priority.

Essay 15

Shrink to Fit

Playing Small

Raise your hand if you've ever been told you were "too" anything. Now put a check mark next to the feedback* you've received from others.

- ☐ Too loud
- ☐ Too tall
- ☐ Too shy
- ☐ Too smart
- ☐ Too big
- ☐ Too afraid
- ☐ Too bold
- ☐ Too intense
- ☐ Too short
- ☐ Too sure of yourself
- ☐ Too old
- ☐ Too brazen
- ☐ Too fat

- ☐ Too effervescent
- ☐ Too progressive
- ☐ Too unappreciative
- ☐ Too outspoken
- ☐ Too political
- ☐ Too controversial
- ☐ Too small
- ☐ Too honest
- ☐ Too lazy
- ☐ Too flirtatious
- ☐ Too complicated
- ☐ Too sophisticated
- ☐ Too elegant

*Feedback can be 'dumping' in disguise. Honest feedback supports and encourages us in our goals. Dumping, on the other hand, is when someone's emotional triggers are set off when this person is around you and she or he holds you responsible for his or her feelings. In the name of 'feedback' s(he) makes you wrong so s(he) doesn't have to feel diminished. Feedback feels good. Dumping feels bad.

☐ Too picky
☐ Too stupid
☐ Too communicative
☐ Too emotional
☐ Too young
☐ Too dark
☐ Too nice
☐ Too bitchy
☐ Too fast
☐ Too cocky
☐ Too envious
☐ Too successful
☐ Too sensitive
☐ Too sexual
☐ Too sick
☐ Too sneaky
☐ Too cerebral

☐ Too spiritual
☐ Too aggressive
☐ Too pretty
☐ Too tenacious
☐ Too enthusiastic
☐ Too invincible
☐ Too truthful
☐ Too gifted
☐ Too complacent
☐ Too quirky
☐ Too outrageous
☐ Too old-fashioned
☐ Too difficult
☐ _____
☐ _____
☐ _____
☐ _____

Congratulations! Those of you who have spent your entire lives not fitting in, not conforming, not complying, not being satisfied, not compromising, not acquiescing, not rolling over, not pretending, not lying about who you are, not trying to please the whole world, and not playing small, have succeeded in finding your way to a place (this book) that celebrates you and your chutzpah. It takes a lot of courage and a high invincibility factor to be yourself. And you did it!

To those of you who haven't quite managed this yet, welcome just the same, you're on your way! After all, we'd never ask you to join us just to fit in.

Think, for a moment, about fitting in. Into what? It's a mold, a perception that someone else or a group of someone elses decided was appropriate for you. Do you know these people? Do you respect these people? Do want to emulate these people? Just what I thought. No, no, and no. And you care about their opinion why? Oh, for approval! You may want to rethink that.

Have you ever noticed how narrow the bandwidth is of acceptable female behavior? Of course you have! Women are either:

- Too ambitious or not ambitious enough
- Too aggressive or not aggressive enough
- Too collaborative or too autonomous
- Too strong or too weak
- Too masculine or too feminine
- Too left brain or too right brain
- Too smart or too dumb
- Too young or too old
- Too assertive or too compliant
- Too confident or too insecure
- Too threatening or too wishy-washy

- Too general or too specific
- Too attractive or too unattractive
- Too business-oriented or too-family oriented
- Too detail-oriented or too big picture oriented
- Too directional or too hands-off
- Too intellectual or too emotional
- _____
- _____
- _____
- _____

■ ■ ■

Last year I had the privilege of speaking at a women's empowerment event. We were talking about this very subject of women being "too" and a women popped up out of her seat, bubbly as can be, to share this story. Terri was a vice president for a national bank and, after only a year with the organization she had the largest book at the bank—her specialty was high wealth individuals. Her manager had recently sat her down and told her she was too effervescent. Can you imagine? It would seem to me that he should have bought her a car or a cruise if she was breaking records in an economic downturn, instead of asking her to calm it down. One would have to wonder what was going on in his life such that "effervescence" was a trigger for him.

Of course, Terri is not alone! In July 2007, Catalyst released a study, _The Double-Bind Dilemma for Women in Leadership: Damned if You Do, Doomed if You Don't_ in which they explored gender stereotyping in corporate leadership. The study concluded that no matter how women lead, they will have limited, conflicting, and frequently unfavorable options that leave them in a "double bind and no-win" dilemma. They observed that:

1. Women leaders are perceived as "never just right"; that is, too soft or too tough.
2. Women leaders are expected to meet higher standards than their male counterparts, and are not justly rewarded for doing so.
3. Women leaders are perceived as competent and not personable when they adopt a stereotypical male leadership style, *or* they are liked but not seen as having valued leadership skills when they adopt a stereotypical female leadership style.

These results accentuate the need for women to define leadership from their unique perspective.

> We do not need to lead like men. We do not need to lead like women. We need to lead like ourselves, and the only way to do that is to *not shrink to fit*.

We must be who we are in a way that suits us *and* the organizations to whom we report. This requires two vital and related skills: self-trust and self-confidence, both of which progressively increase given the time and ample practice.

■ ■ ■

There are two requirements for becoming invincible:

1. Do not shrink to fit.
2. Become more of who you already are.

On the do-not-shrink-to-fit front, I recall that my mother and I once had a brief conversation about what time I'd be arriving at Aunt Rose's house for a Jewish holiday. I told Mom that I wouldn't be attending that year. She was horrified. Not attending! Everyone will talk! This is what I told her: "Everyone will talk about me anyway, regardless of what I do. If I don't attend, then at least one of us will be happy." "Oh," she said.

There comes a time in every woman's life when she realizes that the choice for how she will live the rest of her years is entirely dependent upon her personal vision and preferences. You have arrived at that time in your life.

The truth? You are never, ever, ever, going to fit in! And *"that is a cause for celebration, not an apology."* You will never make anyone completely happy: That is not your job, it is theirs. Therefore, the only person who can absolutely, positively, be happy with who you are, with what you do, with every itty-bitty delicious detail about you, will be *you!* You might as well start now.

Fitting in requires that we get small, that we compromise, that we become less authentic, less powerful than we are. Fitting in implies that we change some aspect(s) of who we worked so hard to reveal, so that others won't feel uncomfortable comparing themselves to us (and feel diminished by the comparison). And if we do know these people, and they want us to shrink to fit in, then we must ask ourselves if these are really the kind of friends we should have anyway.

Suffice it to say that the moment we are required to fit in, we will be asked to forfeit some precious part of ourselves that we have spent most of our lives cultivating. We are asked to do this so that other people aren't inconvenienced into expanding their views of themselves and their world. We are asked to do this so that other people don't have to revamp their perspective. We are asked to do this because, for the most part, people are unmotivated to grow and relinquish their outdated expectations.

People who want to change us so they are more comfortable aren't comfortable with themselves, which means that the minute you change, they'll want you to change again. Exhausting! Repeat after me: Bye. Bye.

Now, for the second ingredient in that formula for invincibility: This is the easy and fun part! This is where you get to take everything you love about yourself, that you are complimented on, that makes you successful and happy, and increase it tenfold—get effervescent about it, while you're at it!

> *"Get more of what you want by becoming more of who you are."*
> —Nancy D. Solomon

This piece requires that you dig deep into your personal treasure chest and mine for all the jewels you may have relinquished over the years in order to accommodate everyone but yourself. It means that you'll become more intimate with yourself and more engaged in your life, and have more choice about the impact you have. It means that you're perfect exactly as you are and the only thing that you need to *do* is let the world in on the secret that you are. Nice to see you!

Initiate Impact!

1. In what area(s) in your life have you been told that you need to 'shrink to fit' in order to be accepted?
2. Is there a common theme when you look at the "too" list at the beginning of this essay?
3. Is the feedback accurate and supportive or is this a reflection of something else?
4. How can you use the wisdom from this exercise to increase your invincibility?
5. What do you think would happen if you let yourself be who you are all the time?
6. How could you use your personal power to change this situation?

Essay 16

I Can't Believe She Did That!

Women and Relationships

> "Of course I didn't tell her. I didn't want her to think
> I was a bitch."
>
> "I didn't want to hurt her feelings."
>
> "I didn't actually lie about why she didn't get the contract.
> I just left out parts of the story so she wouldn't feel bad."
>
> "What good would it do to tell her what really happened;
> there wasn't anything she could do about it anyway."

Women are great at relationships. End of story.

Or is it?

What if there was a seldom-read chapter that told quite a different tale? One that had a more unsavory interpretation, and a less familiar conclusion? And what if that untold passage spoke of collusion, betrayal, and duplicity? What if the fine print detailed the indiscretions of the same relationships that we are reputed to be so protective of? How then would the story end?

The stereotype is that relationships are women's raison d'être. It is assumed, however incorrectly, that our identities are synonymous with relationship. Just as we are "supposed to" want to bear children, we are also supposed to be great at relating, connecting, loving, nurturing, and caring. It is presumed, by both genders, that we will publicly present as kind, considerate, compassionate, and collaborative.

Popular convention aside, it is likely that the number of women to whom this description would not apply is equal to the number to whom it would. We all know women who can be catty, bitchy, condescending, bullying, unsupportive, and downright mean to other women; women who, on their way up the leadership ladder, step on the rung below them rather than lift other women as they climb. We can only guess why. I, for one, have certainly been on the receiving end of those claws more than once and have been dismayed and disillusioned more than angry or upset.

It's not unheard of for us to wear those labels either, is it? Whether earned or not. When we present as strong, powerful, invincible, and in charge, or when autonomy overrides collaboration, and "no" vetoes "yes." When we don't fit in, or when we choose to stand out, raise our hand for recognition, or expose our ambition. When we do anything that is outside of "acceptable female behavior," the response from our female acquaintances is, inevitably, "I can't believe she did that!" Their exclamation means one of two things:

a. I am so proud of you for breaking the mold and setting a new standard for the rest of us. Or
b. How dare you step outside the invisible boundaries and violate the unspoken agreement among women. Now that you've done this, others will expect me to be exceptional, as well.

What our friends don't realize is that it was harder to do than it was to watch.

> The reason this dichotomy so shocks us is that our reputation for relationship can be in such stark contrast to the reality.

■ ■ ■

Many of the personality traits exalted by our culture are identical to the ones that intrude on, and interfere with, our quest for leadership. The end result is that our most powerful tools are transformed into our greatest weapons. Just as a scalpel is used in the operating room to save a life, a similar instrument can be used in the street to take a life. This is the same double-edged sword surrounding the soft issues for which we are famed. Our relationship skills are supremely beneficial in helping us to develop long-term, sustainable alliances that result in positive, high impact, and measurable bottom line results—thus making them a remarkable tool. This almost religious allegiance to relationship, however, is the same thing that thwarts our leadership efforts.

> The trap door is that societal expectation of our role in relationship is exactly what stands in our way when the leadership stakes are highest.

How is that? Think about how challenging it is for us to step up, move forward, or speak out if we even suspect that someone else's feelings might be at risk: Impossible! In this scenario, the relationship dynamic that, a moment ago, contributed to collaboration and team building, now renders this same skill-set an unwitting weapon preventing us from seeking the promotions or leadership positions we've been primed for.

"You cannot be part of the group you're trying to lead." So, we can either be part of a group and be considered collaborative, or poise ourselves for a position of power, which would separate us from the group, thereby making us an outsider or "other." One could say that, in this fashion, we fall upon our own relationship sword.

I offer you the following scenario that is repeated every day across corporate America and in small businesses.

A new group of professional women join together to work on a project. Initially everyone plays nicely. Relationships are formed, alliances are built, conversations flow, and everyone appears to be one nice, big, happy family. The women bond like Krazy Glue and are tickled with their ability to "get it," to understand one another, and to act differently (read that—better, more mature, less aggressive) than the guys do. Then, lo and behold, some crisis (big or small, real or perceived) occurs in which the potential arises for someone to get her feelings hurt.

The situation may involve one woman taking the lead over another. It may involve a promotion or a demotion. Perhaps someone lost the client, alienated the client, or disappointed the client and committed the unforgivable act of letting the team down. The culprit is now considered "other" or "toxic" because she had the audacity to disrupt (unintentionally or not) the status quo and shatter the illusion that everyone was playing nicely together.

Is this unusual? No. Is it a challenge? Yes. Someone must deliver the devastating news that the vault has been violated, and that unpleasant feelings have surfaced. No one, and I mean no one, wants that job.

> There isn't a woman worth her pantyhose who wants to be responsible for pointing a finger, demanding accountability, and saying not-so-nice words that will make both women feel quite uncomfortable. At least not in public.

Here are the possibilities for this situation:

A. No one says anything and everyone hopes it will go away or the perpetrator will somehow, by osmosis, realize the error of her ways and apologize in advance of any accusation.

B. Everyone will talk about this woman behind her back, but act as though everything is no big deal to her face. The rest of the group will, at a later time, collectively remark that they can't believe "she doesn't even get it." At this point the poor woman now becomes socially demoted to the status of 'not one of us', and is relegated to the hopeless category. No one will even eat lunch with her except on the occasion when they want to leech gossip.

C. She gets demoted, real time.

D. Some brave soul takes her aside and fills her in on the situation. This woman suffers the humiliation of knowing that everyone had been talking about her all this time, but no one had been willing to tell her the truth to her face. Said woman now feels demoralized, devalued, minimized, betrayed, and embarrassed beyond recovery. She leaves the organization and, around the water cooler, her former colleagues claim that they don't get why she walked off in a huff.

I have personally witnessed this sequence of events countless times, and I have coached women on both sides of this blade. The result? No one wins. At the end of the day, everyone has unnecessarily been compromised.

In most cases, a little bit of courage would have gone a very long way. Now, the details as betrayer or betrayed may vary, but what is fairly consistent is the inability or unwillingness of one woman to honestly, and without malice, give another woman constructive, pertinent feedback. Few women willingly tell the truth when it comes to delivering news that will, in any way, stir up unhappy, negative, or unwelcome feelings. We are expert at saying the right thing, saying the nice thing, complimenting, acknowledging, complaining, and whining so long as no one gets her feelings rearranged. Some of us are expert at passive-aggressive behavior.

It is not uncommon to observe connection-driven female professionals who betray themselves in the name of some relationships, while subjugating themselves in others. Often these women weren't conscious of what they were doing, and they ended up resenting the hell out of those so-called friends who bore witness to their self-defeating ways and did nothing to intervene. "How could you let me do this to myself?"

This epidemic disempowerment, is killing our collective female spirit, making mockery of our claims to leadership and rendering us hypocrites of the worse kind. We see our sisters mimic our behavior and either we don't say anything because we don't want to hurt their feelings or, even more abhorrently, we see it but in our efforts to hinder their advancement we hold tight to our thoughts. Ugly!

> So what transpires when the very things at which we excel have the dual function of holding us back and placing our personal power in abeyance?

When our greatest attribute becomes our greatest liability? When the sharpest edge of our greatest tool rips into the flesh of our power, becoming a sinister weapon?

Nothing good, I can tell you that.

■ ■ ■

When the valued qualities that have become synonymous with women leaders are the very same ones that we unconsciously (and, in all likelihood, unintentionally) use to disempower ourselves, we unwittingly disqualify ourselves from the very roles we seek. We then find ourselves wondering why we're not receiving due recognition or why we're stagnant in our careers and in our lives.

If we are to embrace integrity as our own, then we must be intimately familiar with how we use, abuse, or misuse our relationship skills, and how that impacts our ability to powerfully and successfully impact the world. We must carefully scrutinize what we are doing to ourselves and, in the process, doing to those around us. We need to investigate ways in which we can preserve our relationships without becoming doormats. We must learn how to speak our truth without pretense of weakness or wiles. Perhaps when it is least easy to do so, we must learn how to speak up for ourselves while trusting that our colleagues will do the same.

> When we curtail our power to make someone feel comfortable, or when we dilute or alter our opinions for fear of reprisal, we are, in essence, playing God.

Manipulating circumstances (by omission or commission) so that others don't have to deal with their potential feelings implies that we think they can't handle them. Ultimately it says, "I create my own reality, but I don't trust that you create yours. Since I'm afraid you can't handle your feelings, I'm going to tamper with the situation so you don't have to deal with the truth." This is a distant cousin to the positive impact we can be proud of, and to the invincibility we deserve.

We are, clichés aside, the guardian of our relationships. That gift comes bundled with a responsibility: That responsibility is to the truth. Impact is bred from our relationship with ourselves. Our character is who we are. Our reputation is what others think of us. We really don't want to contribute to the negative PR of what it means to be a woman, do we? We really don't want to be in a situation where we find ourselves saying, "I can't believe I said that!" do we?

Initiate Impact!

1. If you were to change one thing about how you relate to other women, what would it be?
    - How would that alter the way you impact your relationships?
    - How would that alter the way your relationships impact you?
2. In what ways could you lift other women up the corporate ladder that you're climbing?
3. What strategic relationships do you need to cultivate within your organization?
4. How would mentoring the women behind you positively impact your organization?
    - How would it impact you?

Essay 17

Your Inner Bag Lady

Money and Power

Rumor has it that you and I have a mortal fear of becoming bag ladies.

Stop laughing. Of course, we already knew that! I count myself among many financially savvy, educated, influential, and professional women who harbor this same anxiety. We keep it in our secret closet, right alongside our imposter syndrome. (It's a parallel conversation.) We live that fear every day of our lives, don't we? And before it was ours, it was our mother's fear; and before that, her mother's.

It's a curious expenditure of energy, don't you think? Here we are, equipped to have babies, negotiate contracts, collaborate with colleagues, rise through the ranks of leadership, manage large teams of people, and—at the end of the day—get that last load of laundry done. We accomplish these things without hesitation or ambivalence.

Yet when it comes to our personal finances, many of us find ourselves off in a dark corner, marinating in a pool of fear.

We fret. We unravel at the seams. We agonize. We procrastinate. We avoid. We deny. We do everything *but* manage our money. I spoke with an attorney the other day who told me that, perhaps, *only*

10 percent of her female clients are financially prepared in the event of their death. Not good!

■ ■ ■

In 2006, Allianz Life Insurance Company of North America commissioned *The Allianz Women, Money and Power Study* in an attempt to better understand the unique relationship we women have with our finances. Here's what they discovered.

- ◆ 48 percent of women earning $100K+ fear becoming a bag lady.
- ◆ 46 percent of *all* women fear becoming a bag lady.
- ◆ 90 percent of all women feel financially insecure.
- ◆ 3 percent of editorial content in women's magazines is dedicated to the subject of personal finance.

Wow!

One out of two of us are frightened to death that, at some point, we will discover that our pockets are empty—and we won't have any way to refill them. We know that it's irrational thinking. We know that we're personally powerful, and that if we did it before (whatever *it* might be: made the money, got the job, bought the house, etc.), then we can do it again. Nonetheless, we still go to bed at night dreading the thought of waking up penniless, homeless, and powerless.

The Allianz study revealed that our anxiety is attributable to a number of significant social influences. For instance:

- ◆ Women live as much as one third of their lives in retirement.
- ◆ Women can't rely on Social Security anymore.
- ◆ Women outlive men by an average of seven years.
- ◆ Divorce rate projections exceed 50 percent.
- ◆ Women lack financial education. (Few parents spend time teaching financial independence to their daughters—18 percent of mothers and 4 percent of fathers give their daughters a financial education.)

Each one of these cultural anxieties results from women placing their financial health in the hands of the man in their life, whether it is their husband, their father, or even the government.

There are many factors that impede women from assuming full financial responsibility for themselves and their families. Extended family obligations as well as inequitable wages are at the top of a very long list. These challenges continue to be addressed by women; Until we've made much more progress toward resolving these issues, we will continue to be reliant on "other" for our finances and, therefore, our power.

These societal conditions do not, however, preclude you from taking every step within your power to be the guardian of your finances. Maybe you can't earn a six-figure income, but maybe you can get a minimum wage job and stash away some money. Maybe you can't rely on Social Security, but that doesn't mean that you cannot rely on yourself. Maybe your family failed to provide you with a financial education, but reading these words right now should tell you that you are perfectly capable of filling in the gaps in your learning.

■ ■ ■

The legitimacy and impact of the conclusions drawn from this study are undeniable. *But they are not the whole story.* The issues are much deeper and more organic than these sociological factors would suggest. As valid as they are, these points are symptomatic of a more systemic and pervasive phenomenon: *the relationship women have with their personal power.*

Money is power. The current, however, doesn't necessarily flow the other way: You *can* certainly be powerful and not have money. You can also have lots of money and be personally disempowered. Regardless of whether you and I agree with this paradigm, it is a global fact of life.

Have you ever wondered why so many women have a convoluted, emotionally drenched relationship with their finances? It is for the very same reasons that we ceaselessly wrestle with our personal power (see Essay #24).

You'll take a giant step toward being invincible when you complete the money and power exercise in Figure 17.1. Look at one column at a time, (begin with money) and place a check in the boxes that best

	MONEY	PERSONAL POWER
I have it intermittently.		
I envy others who have it.		
I squander it.		
I misuse it or abuse it.		
I have healthy boundaries around it.		
I give it away more than I keep it.		
I compare mine to others'.		
I let others take it from me.		
I hoard it, spending as little as I can get away with.		
I can't seem to hold onto it.		

FIGURE 17.1 Money and Personal Power

describe you. Then do the same thing with the personal power column (concealing the money column with a bookmark). *Go with your gut and don't over think the statements or your response to them.*

- ◆ What pattern do you see? With money? With your personal power?
- ◆ What does the pattern tell you about yourself?
- ◆ Is your relationship with one or both of these steady, solid, and dependable?
- ◆ Does it flip-flop all over the place, depending what else is going on?
- ◆ What impact does this pattern have on your life and on your career?
- ◆ What would you like to change?
- ◆ How will that change impact your life?

> *"What we do with our money is what we do with our power."*
> —Nancy D. Solomon

The implications? If you want to live your retirement in great comfort; if you want a healthy marriage; if you want to be self-sufficient—whatever it is that you want is reliant upon that core relationship with yourself and with your personal power. Therein lies the secret to forever banishing that bag lady who lives inside your head.

We need to promise ourselves that these explanations for our behavior will never be allowed to be turned into excuses—just because a study reports that we feel threatened by the possibility of becoming bag ladies, it doesn't imply that we have to sit back on our haunches and let our lives happen to us. If anything, this study is a wake-up call, a veritable report card indicating where we need to focus our emotional and mental resources. Let's use it that way.

The very second we become aware that we are using these explanations to hide—to pretend we are not as authentically powerful as we actually are—then these "reasons" are transformed into mechanisms for diminishing our power, our purpose, and our passion. And at that point, they are merely lame justifications for not having positive impact.

The cultural conditions and stereotypes with which you were raised were not created by you. We are, however, accountable for perpetuating them. None of us can change every situation in our lives; but what we *do* have control over is our reaction to those situations. When we strengthen the connection we have with our intrinsic power, the same factors discovered in the Allianz study may continue to influence us, but we will react to and behave differently as a result of owning our power.

This is the sharpest edge of the issue, and the sharpest edge of *every* issue we face: ***Owning our personal power equips us to positively impact our lives and the world.***

When we take even the most peripheral view of women in society, what we discover is that little girls, who eventually grow into women who participate in studies, are still weaned on the myth of Prince Charming. The majority of us continue to be indoctrinated with the idea that if we're patient enough, thin enough, compliant enough, sexy enough, _____ *He* will, eventually, show up.

When he arrives, your knight might be tattered and torn. He may have a fidelity issue, drinking problem, or drug addiction. He may have worked himself through four marriages, which, poor thing, left him no time or energy to work at a job. No matter; he fulfills your most basic requirement, even if his armor is tarnished or missing: He's breathing. And given the alternative—that you will take full responsibility for your own financial health—he's looking mighty good.

Barbara Stanny has written several valuable books on this subject. My favorites are: *The Secrets of Six-Figure Women: Surprise Strategies to Up Your Earnings and Change Your Life* (HarperCollins, 2002); and *Prince Charming Isn't Coming: How Women Get Smart About Money* (Penguin, 2007).

Humor and sarcasm aside, each and every one of you reading these words has experienced your own version of this story, or know a woman very close to you who has. We have been acculturated to look outside ourselves for our worth. So much of our merit is calculated by outward appearances; by the image we present to the world; the partner we're with; the house we live in; the car we drive; our job description; _____; and all other matters concerned with how our lives appear. *Note:* Although this is a conversation about money and power, I want to emphasize that our health and our friends determine our wealth, not the balance in our checkbook. I know we already know this, but a gentle reminder is always nice.

Are you as disturbed as I am that only 3 percent of editorial content in women's magazines is dedicated to the subject of personal finance? That means that we spend more time learning about how to wax, tweeze, and color our hair than we do planning for the one third of our lives that we'll live in retirement. It implies that we'll spend more time figuring out how to talk to our lover, our boss, our mother, and our children, than we do talking ourselves out of credit card debt.

What's most alarming is that, in our hear-me-roar voice, we take our 77 cents on the dollar straight to the magazine stands where we purchase the literature that perpetuates negative female stereotypes, warns us about environmental issues such as nasty underarm odor, and in the same breath, reminds us that we can have it all. End of rant.

■ ■ ■

So what is the dynamic stimulated by this outward focus, by disowning our personal power?

This is a *HUGE* question!

We end up thinking that the sum of money that we earn, save, or spend magically appeared in our lives without our involvement: Someone or something else delivered it to our door. What is the unfortunate consequence of internalizing this concept?

If we aren't aware of our role in this—if we are not responsible for what has "magically" appeared in our lives—then these things can effortlessly disappear without our participation as well.

In other words: If we don't "own" the power that created the money, then we don't feel responsible for it. (Think: We get more value from a personal development workshop that *we* pay for.) If we don't feel like we had anything, whatsoever, to do with *making* the money; then we won't have anything to do with it disappearing either—so it can vanish into thin air just as easily as it arrived.

And voilà—we are bag ladies!

You can be assured that we are much less likely to succumb to bag lady status when we build our inner wealth—the internal resources we need to be fully empowered. Reading this book is a powerful step in that direction. Doing the exercises at the end of each essay will help you to get the wisdom "in your bones." Here are some practical ideas, in abbreviated form, to assist you to make some hefty deposits in your invincibility account:

♦ Surround yourself with people who already have what you want: In this case, financial wealth and freedom. Ask questions that will empower you to empower yourself. If you don't know what those are, ask your new wealthy friends what questions *they* asked. Take good notes.

♦ You taught yourself how to salsa, sing, and sew, which means you're also smart enough to learn how to read a balance sheet and a profit and loss statement. It's easier than getting along with your relatives. You can definitely handle this!

♦ Now that it is no longer a secret that so many women have a less than ideal relationship with money, many fabulous resources have become available. Books, classes, and seminars will educate you and help you build a new network of financially savvy friends. My suggestion? Treat yourself to a copy of Mikelann Valterra's (founding director of the Women's Earning Institute) *"Why Women Earn Less: How to Make What You're Really Worth"* (Career Press, 2004). Now that's personal power!

♦ Your net worth is not your self-worth. Your self-worth has far more value than any number in your bank account. Take a personal inventory of your beliefs, values, and goals with as much enthusiasm as you have for ordering shoes online or take-out sushi. Then come up with a strategy more concrete than just hoping that your financial situation will work itself out.

♦ You have already amounted to something pretty great. You have forgotten more successes than you can remember, and while it is true that your friends are your wealth, it would be nice to have the means to take them on a cruise around the world. You are what you think. Focus on scarcity and you will create lack. Focus on your financial goals, and you'll exceed them in record time.

♦ Repeat this personal empowerment mantra until you don't need to: "If it's to be, it's up to me."

> There are going to be days when you doubt your ability to manifest anything more than trouble. During those times remember: *"you are not the problem you have."*
>
> —Nancy D. Solomon

Periodically you *will* have relapses where you envision yourself in a filthy housedress, wearing rolled-to-the-ankle stockings and being asphyxiated by the plastic bags overflowing from your shopping cart – the very same cart that pulls up to your mental curb and defies you to send it away–do that!

P.S. The Allianz Study found that the majority of men find financially secure women to be very sexy. Now *that* might be motivation, ladies.

Initiate Impact!

1. How will a change in your relationship between money and your personal power transform the way you impact the world?

2. In what ways does your relationship to money impact your ability to do your job?

3. In what ways does your work (paid or volunteer) contribute to and reinforce your beliefs about your personal power?

4. If you were motivated to improve your self-esteem, how would you need to alter your relationship to your finances?

Essay 18

Life's Too Short to Wear Ugly Shoes
Depression and Anxiety

Alcoholism, drug abuse, domestic violence, depression, anxiety.

Not just on the streets anymore, but in the cubicle next to yours at the office. Looking at the work culture through a purely statistical lens, there is only one conclusion that can be drawn: We are not doing great. Signs of personal distress are plastered all over the walls of small businesses and corporate America; the most prevalent and costly of all is depression.[1] Yes, the very same illness that sent someone you know to bed for weeks is also wreaking havoc on America's workforce.

In 2003 the *Journal of Clinical Psychiatry* estimated that the annual cost of depression in the United States was $83.1 billion, $51.5 billion of which is loss of workplace productivity—not in absenteeism but in *presenteeism*: Employees may physically show up for work, but are so emotionally and spiritually bankrupt that they not only fail to earn their wages, but exact a toll just by being there. These are likely the "actively disengaged," as identified by the Gallup Organization. You know these people: They show up for work, slither through the day unnoticed, collect their paycheck, and retreat at the very moment the bell rings.

---

[1]It goes without saying that both clinical depression and anxiety are serious illnesses that may require medical and/or psychological intervention. If you experience either of these, or if you're not certain as to the nature of your discomfort, then the most powerful thing you can do is immediately march yourself off to your preferred health practitioner and find out what's going on and what you can do about it.

It is likely that they are too numb to even notice that they are barely tolerating their own lives.

The situation is oversimplified, however, when the workforce is merely segregated into either engaged or disengaged status. The workplace is a microcosm for the world at large, where people make every one of their decisions from one of two distinct, yet equally powerful, vantage points: either to get away from pain (40%), or to go to pleasure (40%). (20% are both towards and away.)

If you step back for a moment to the University of Florida study cited in Essay #33, the research unquestionably concluded that people are, at many levels, in search of emotion-specific experiences.

> It then becomes quite clear that the engaged have made life choices on the side of going to pleasure, while their disengaged counterparts have consistently sought out the escape from pain card.

Engaged people who are attempting to step into their own power are not running away from what they don't want, but are running toward a passion and a purpose. There is reciprocity between both groups, as within any system. That is to say, the engaged impact the disengaged and vice-versa: The ones running toward pleasure influence those aiming to escape pain. This reciprocity creates even more emotions—oh, my gosh, there's no way of getting away from this feeling stuff, is there?

If even superficial emotional exchanges cause people to squirm in their shoes, one can only imagine the blisters raised by the presence of depression in conference room settings. It is not the point of this essay to microscopically examine the multiple factors that are the foundation of depression, but to state the obvious, which is that depression does, indeed, exist in your business, and that takes a deep emotional and financial toll on its psyche.

Depression, in the spiritual sense of the word, can be likened to a French coffee pot. When you press down on the plunger, the coffee rises on all sides of the pot. Similarly, when your core self—your very essence—is stuffed down or stifled in any way, depression seems to be the emotion that arises on all sides of you to let you know that you aren't giving free expression to your spirit.

> Consider this: It is much less likely that you will be depressed if you are doing something that is congruent with your life purpose that, in turn, stimulates the passion within you.

It's worth mentioning here that, for a multitude of reasons, women experience and/or report a much higher incidence of depression than men, and that these same women make up over 50 percent of the American workforce. This brings us back to the point of the Super Software Company story. As I have spent more time with women like those I met that weekend at the retreat (see Essay #11), I've discovered that although many of these women are not diagnosed as clinically depressed, many are suffering from a serious case of French Coffee Press, which translates to: Life looks great and feels lousy.

■ ■ ■

Anxiety is the discrepancy between our mind's desire and God's greatest good for us. It is the space between what the ego demands and what the heart requires. The larger the gap between the two the more anxiety juice that flows. Anxiety is a sign that we are off-purpose; that our head has thought us into a corner that we can't find our way out of. Anxiety can be compared to a smoke detector—you want the detector's alarm to sound well before the fire is out of control. Similarly, anxiety is our body's way of letting us know that all is not peaceful, calm, and well in our world—that something we're either thinking or doing is counterproductive to our purpose, to our intention, or to our very livelihood.

I have met very few people who were uncontrollably anxious and on purpose at the same time. When we are on purpose we are using our God-given gifts and talents and we are experiencing passion. Passion is the heart's antidote for anxiety.

Most of us experience some degree of anxiety every day. We may get anxious when we're running late for a meeting, when we're not prepared for said meeting, when our senior management will be at the meeting, and when there are 50 other things we'd rather do than attend the meeting.

Spiritual anxiety results from being off purpose and, therefore, from being disempowered.

Think back to a time when you knew you could be meditating, but you were cleaning instead; when you felt the sensation of your inner wisdom urging you to write in your journal, but you called a friend instead; or when you clearly heard the message to do one thing and, avoiding it, did something else. All these instances were likely to have produced anxiety in you. Why? Because your greater light, your instincts, knew that it would serve your best and highest good to do something other than what you were doing. Voilà! Anxiety, which can be compared to anti-virus software on your computer letting you know in advance that there is something more to be discovered.

Perhaps you're wondering what depression and anxiety have to do with impact, invisibility, and invincibility. They are astonishingly intertwined! Think about this:

◆ Depression is a symptom of being off purpose.
◆ Depression leads us to be off purpose.
◆ When we're depressed, we feel invisible.
◆ When we're depressed, we place our invincibility on hold.
◆ When we're depressed, we're unable to create positive impact.
◆ Anxiety is a signal that impact is within our reach.
◆ Anxiety is a sign that our invincibility is still an option.

If you're in the garden, you can expect some weeds. What's the message here? If you're aiming for impact, you can expect some unpleasant encounters with your ego, with depression, and with anxiety.

These are merely circumstances. You have depression. *You* aren't depression. You have anxiety. *You* aren't anxiety. *"You are not the problem you have."* It is merely one aspect of a zillion other things going on in your life right now. We choose how we walk through our lives. How do you want to walk in yours?

Initiate Impact!

1. Think back to a time in your career when you felt down or depressed. How did that impact your ability to do your job?
2. Was this down or depressed phase triggered by something at work, in your career?
   - In your personal life?
3. How did you resolve those feelings?
   - Was there a correlation between how you felt and what you were doing?
4. What did you learn about yourself?
   - How can you apply this wisdom to your life the next time you feel off or not as on purpose and happy as you'd like?

Part Four

What Increases Impact?

Essay 19

Ten Carats

Mining Your Treasures

If you only read one chapter in this book, make it this one.

Have you ever wondered why some women are successful and others are not? Successful, of course, refers to getting what you want, on your terms, if not in your timing. If an advanced degree was part of your vision, and you earned it, then you are successful. If making a certain income was a goal of yours, and you reached it, then you are successful. If you wanted to leave behind your high profile job and stay home to take care of your children, and you have managed to do that, then you are successful.

What I've found to be true is that for the most part people can be sorted into two well-defined groups: Those who are getting *it* done and those who are talking about getting it done: Those who seek their success and those who are waiting for their success to show up. There is only *one* difference between the two—permission. Successful women are those who are getting it done because they have given themselves permission to be powerful. They have given themselves permission to stand out, leave the herd, live with the discomfort, and wrestle with the fear that keeps company with courage.

> "Permission is the single most vital component for getting what you want out of your professional and personal life."

Regardless of which group you identify with today, you can be positive that at some point you did something you'd categorize as successful. Can you recall a time when you gave yourself permission to turn off the environmental noise; to sit quietly with yourself and heed that soft voice within you? To hear her wisdom guide you to your next success?

- What happened immediately prior to that time?
- Were you simply finished with where you were?
- Had things gotten too hard?
- Was life more painful than you wanted it to be?
- Did you make this change at someone else's suggestion?

Knowing the answers to these questions will provide you with a hint of how you transition from phase to phase in your life; use that identical formula next time you're moving through a transformative stage in your evolution.

Want to know the best-kept secret of successful women? Women who are living powerfully are not necessarily more talented than the other group. They don't have greater skills or a higher IQ either. (Truth be told, sometimes the really smart ones think themselves out of their greatness by doing the logical, rational, practical thing.) They aren't more ambitious than the other group. They're not prettier, thinner, wealthier, more politically savvy, or more sophisticated than the other group. The solitary differentiating factor is that the ones who are getting it done have given themselves permission to do everything they've penciled in on their life's agenda. No matter what!

> Those of us who are getting it done live our lives as unapologetically as any woman possibly can; and that alone is one of our most impressive accomplishments.

We have given ourselves permission to take up space, to relinquish the shelter of our invisibility, to move freely about in our own skin. We allow ourselves to be seen, heard, and celebrated: To be us! We defend our inalienable right to ask others and ourselves the super charged questions; especially the huge ones that help us grow and evolve. We make the assumption that we are entitled to use the gifts that we were given; and naturally assume that others will treasure the impact those gifts have on the world. We're like a golden retriever, who just assumes that we are always thrilled to see her (which we are).

What's interesting is that we may not even be particularly dialed into the permission factor; most of the time we don't even realize that permission is what we've granted ourselves until we're far down the road, or someone else points it out to us. Laurie in Essay #6 was cognizant of the role that self-permission played in her decision to trade her corporate ID in for diapers and sleepless nights. She talked about it often, and consciously dismantled the beliefs that precluded her from giving herself the requisite permission she needed to make such a bold choice.

> Permission. *"Because life treats us as we treat it."*
> —Nancy D. Solomon

In order to fulfill the promise of our life purpose, we need to put our old beliefs in quarantine. These old friends are like tattered and torn slippers; we don't want to discard them because they're shaped to our feet, have supported us through our journey, and, though worn out and ragged, their habitual and familiar fit is very comforting.

> It can feel abnormal to trespass the cultural norms we've inherited.

The moment we give ourselves permission to download the latest version of ourselves, we're suddenly on our own, with no role model in sight, doing the things the people who love us most might have told us we couldn't or shouldn't be doing. To say nothing of the fact that we're still surrounded by women who don't necessarily see those old norms as a problem.

These women who are getting it done deal with the same issues all women do; they just don't allow those issues to dominate their lives because they know that they are more powerful than the issues they have.

It's both our right and our responsibility to give ourselves permission to live our lives on purpose and to leave our impact behind. Permission creates impact by opening up our treasure vault and inviting every jewel within us to come out; to be as big, bodacious and brazen as we dare (Think: ten carats).

Initiate Impact!

1. What do you want to give yourself permission to do?
   - How long have you wanted this?
   - What's holding you back?
   - What beliefs do you hold that stand in your way?
   - Who do you know who would be your champion for this?
2. Who is a role model in your life who gave herself or himself permission?
   - What did she or he put down in order to pick this up?
   - What was his or her biggest challenge?
   - In what ways are you most like him or her?

Essay 20

Yadda, Yadda, Yadda and Blah, Blah, Blah

Getting It Done

Boring, empty talk.

While many people have the potential for doing something of considerable consequence, something with measurable impact, there are far more of us talking about doing whatever *it* is, than those of us who are actually getting it done. Let's call these two contrasting groups "The Doers" and "The Yaddas," shall we?

One day I was having a conversation with a British colleague about this very subject. Out loud, he wondered why we Americans spend so much time and energy on the conversation around our projects, rather than on completing the projects themselves. I am witness to the remarkable volume of quality work he produces daily, and have been intrigued by his ability to say it, do it, and get on to the next thing.

Talk is cheap. Really cheap.

Jonathan's life looks much different than mine on the outside, which made it convenient, not too long into our conversation, for me to mentally drag out the excuses as to why he is so accomplished and

123

I am so exhausted. More than once I'd observed that while he is working on his projects I'm over thinking mine. An example of this? I *thought* about writing this book for five years: I *wrote* it in three months.

Talking is not a commitment. Action is.

Note: Very few of us lie neatly in either "The Doers" or "The Yaddas" category. As a matter of fact, throughout our lives we may switch back and forth between the two groups: Like everything else our potential contracts and expands and although it has a set point, it is subject to change through our intervention.

There are a multitude of reasons we fail to turn our brilliant ideas, our intellectual capital, into actionable items and bottom line results. The two biggies are, predictably, fear (90 percent) and timing (10 percent).

Everyone experiences fear. "The Doers" have the identical fears as "The Yaddas" folks. And the quantity of fear doesn't vary much between the groups, either. I know, I know, all of us have met people who claim to be fearless. My industry is saturated with them. There are dozens of books on the shelves declaring that we should live a fearless life, have fear no more, and banish fear from our lives once and for all. Yadda, yadda, yadda and blah, blah, blah!

---

*"If someone tells you they don't have any fear, they
are lying to both of you."*
—Nancy D. Solomon

These books were written by people who drank the *"If I say it positively enough any fool will believe me"* Kool Aid. It is not only impossible to banish fear from your life, it is undesirable as well. Doing so, as though that were actually possible, would be akin to taking the batteries out of the smoke detectors in your home. Fear is an indicator of one of two things: Either there's a bear running you up a tree in the woods, or you're experimenting with the stuff you're made of, with your courage quotient. Regarding the former, congratulations that you're alive to read this. As to the latter, congratulations that you're willing to pursue your purpose and passion even though you might not have a map to this uncharted territory.

Here's the deal: If you're alive, then, by all means, live! *Fear is part of your path, not separate from it.* Probably one of the beliefs most unsupportive of living your purpose, to finding your passion, to giving yourself permission to have real impact, is that having fear indicates something is not right. No, no, no, no. That is absolutely *not* the case. If you're on purpose you're going to have fear. As a matter of fact, you can't be on purpose without it. Why? Because fear is your body's cue that you're living large, shifting gears, out of your comfort zone, in your learning zone, and experiencing a bit of exhilaration. Did you know that your body experiences fear and excitement almost identically? True. Elevated heartbeat, sweaty palms, shallow rapid breathing, and dry mouth, to name a few signals.

If you're committed to living a full, rich, impactful life, things aren't going to be peaceful, centered, and light all the time—you can expect to encounter some fear. Learn to enjoy it or, at the very least, appreciate its function in your life.

Yes, we can all benefit from a positive outlook; yes, we can learn to manage our fears; yes, we can even learn to use our fears productively. But that's a far different story than the one saying that you shouldn't have any fear.

Today would be a great day to give up the idea, once and for all, that courageous, powerful, invincible people lack the fear gene. Discarding that thought will make your life infinitely better.

■ ■ ■

So now that you've permanently laid to rest the idea that you're the only one on earth who experiences life-halting fear, let's take a look at what differentiates the people who are "The Doers" from those who are "The Yaddas."

Those in "The Doer" group certainly notice fear when it comes up in their minds and in their bodies. It, undoubtedly, becomes *part* of their decision-making process; but it is only one of many factors they consider when making their eventual choice.

"The Yaddas" notice their fear in the same way, except for two things:

1. The fear becomes *it* in the decision-making process, obscuring all other factors.
2. The fear becomes anchored to their identity. It becomes *who* they are.

■ ■ ■

The real differentiating factor between the two groups, the most significant distinction, lies in one tiny word:

AND.

The people who are "The Doers" have mastered the use of the word *and*.

- They feel the fear *and* they do it anyway.
- They see the obstacles *and* they see the opportunities.
- They recognize their limitations *and* they're willing to discover the ways in which to work through them or around them.
- They are intimate with their strengths *and* their weaknesses.
- _____
- _____
- _____

Their counterparts, "The Yaddas," have mastered the use of the word

BUT.

- I want to start my own business, *but* I don't know how.
- I would really like that promotion, *but* I'm too shy to ask for it.
- I'd go out with him, *but* I was hurt last time.
- I would save for a new house, *but* it's a lot of money.
- _____
- _____
- _____

Did you see what happened? Did you feel what happened? Using the word *and* throws the doors of possibility wide open. It feels optimistic, breezy, exciting, challenging. *And* is a word of discovery, creativity, and curiosity. The very energy of it assumes that where there is a will there is a way. It takes for granted that whatever we're thinking about will get done. *And* assumes that even if we don't know how to accomplish this now, at some point we know we will.

Over to the other side, we find poor pathetic *but*. The same size word that packs an entirely different punch. *But* slams the door closed. *But* is drenched in excuses. *But* is not only caution, it is pessimism. The deal is done and over with before we even had a chance to explore it. It neutralizes whatever is in front of us. *But* may be fatal.

Are you wondering how you can integrate this theory into your life, in concrete terms that are going to produce results you'll get excited about? Let's pretend that you are seriously contemplating taking the mental leap from "The Yaddas" to "The Doers." The most helpful thing you can do to inspire yourself to action will be for you to establish the connection between your head and your heart. Translated, that means you want to identify what it is about this project or idea (the mental component—your head) that sings to your spirit (the spiritual and emotional components—your heart). What is this project's connection to your life purpose? How will it feel when you "get it done?" These are practical questions that will, eventually, become second nature to you.

You'll want to revisit The Impact Cycle in Essay #6 or do the exercise below. Place your idea or project on the schematic and fill in the five steps.

The Experience: _____

The Emotions: _____

God: _____

Life Purpose: _____

Impact: _____

This will give you a precise picture of how this project relates to your life purpose, *and* if it doesn't. Either way, your life just got a whole lot easier. If there isn't a connection to your life purpose, as my children would say, "Hasta le bye bye." If there is congruency between the project and your life purpose then you have a dozen reasons to take your foot off the brake *and* press the accelerator. Note: Find the speed that will inspire *you*.

Initiate Impact!

1. What excuses do you use for not getting it done?
   - What fears come up in you when you think about getting it done?
2. What's one thing you did in your life that you procrastinated about for years, and then accomplished?
   - What compelled you to take those first steps?
3. How do your fears operate at work?
4. What one thing could you do to decrease your fear and increase your impact?

Essay 21

The 'I' in Invincible

Personal Accountability

Editor: We can't use that title. Invisible and invincible aren't parallel phrases.

Me: What's a parallel phrase?

Editor: It would mean that they're opposites; but the opposite of invisible is *visible*.

Me: Oh, but they *are* opposites! To be invisible means that either we feel powerless or we're treated as though we are powerless, or both. It means that we're taken so lightly that nobody even sees us. Invisible implies that we don't make any difference in the world; that we don't have any impact. We don't even exist! Poof!

Editor: Go on.

Me: To be invincible declares that there isn't anything that can come our way that we won't be able handle. It means that we're indomitable; that our spirit will persist regardless of the obstacles we face. It means that not only are we powerful, but incapable of being defeated. It means we have substance. It means we know that we are worthy and we deserve to take our place in the world and have impact!

Editor: Okay. We'll use it.

■ ■ ■

Businesswoman, publisher, and author Helen Gurley Brown[1] did us boomer babes a great disservice by telling us that we could have it all. She failed to point out that we couldn't have it all *at once*. There are now approximately 40 million of us running around, cookbook in one hand, profit and loss statement in the other, frantically searching for ways to mask the fact that our inner chick feels like a pigeon.

FACT #1: You are a success. Failure and your name don't even belong in the same sentence. We usually don't succeed at the things that either we shouldn't be doing to begin with (because they didn't belong to us), or that we need to practice (because we're on our path). You've had more success that you can possibly keep track of. Surround yourself only with people who see your perfection and celebrate your impact on them! FYI: You cannot succeed at something *and* still be invincible.

FACT #2: You cannot have it all at the same time, although you can have it all. You may want to train for a marathon, learn to speak Italian, replace your assistant, finish that scrapbook, organize your office, network to fill your sales pipeline, and figure out why your soufflés collapse when you take them out of the oven. But you cannot do all of this in one day. Not even if you were Superwoman—who, I'm certain, you would outperform. You can be invincible *and* not want it all; whatever "all" means to you.

■ ■ ■

Invincibility does not imply that you will *never* feel overwhelmed; nor does it suggest that you will never have unexpected outcomes or rip your pantyhose right before a major presentation. It doesn't indicate that everyone will like you; in fact, some people will probably feel intimidated around you. It doesn't even suggest that you won't have days when you, too, feel invisible. It in no way means that unfortunate things won't happen, that you will never fail, and that some days you won't feel like giving up because life got just too much.

---

[1]For those of you who don't know who HGB is, let me say two things: You're probably under the age of 40; she's the founder of *Cosmopolitan* magazine.

To be invincible means that you will handle whatever shows up in your life purposefully and powerfully, even when you don't feel like it. You may not know the answer to every question in front of you, but you know that the answer will appear when the timing is perfect.

Life will still present us with circumstances that we are positive we're not qualified to handle. However, we're certain that although we may not know what to do now, at some point, we will. We invincibles have access to the resources to help us through any situation. If the questions are important enough to us, we'll get them answered.

Being invincible means that we are 100 percent accountable for our lives. It means that we "own" every last thing that's going on—because we know, at some level, that everything that's happening is serving our best and highest good. The task is to figure out what that is; to glean the wisdom from it; to use it to fulfill our life purpose; and to create positive impact. This is an unequivocal universal principle.

If we had a members only club, this be would our charter.

1. *We trust ourselves—(as a rule and with exceptions).*
2. *We know our worth and are unwilling to compromise it (except when we forget, and then we have great friends to remind us).*
3. *We live our values (except when we forget, and then we self-correct)*
4. *We neither diminish who we are nor what we do (ditto #2).*
5. *We know the difference we make (except for the times we're in denial).*
6. *We're committed to becoming more of who we are—without exception.*

Invincibility is a lifestyle choice, a way of being in the world. Its magic lies in the fact that we can relinquish the cloak of invisibility and make the choice to show up invincibly in our lives at any time—in an instant! Like everything else in life, it's a choice.

Something to contemplate: When you're in the midst of making an important decision, one that requires you to be purposeful, powerful and passionate, ask yourself this question:

"Am I running away from my invisibility or am I running toward my invincibility?"
—Nancy D. Solomon

Initiate Impact!

1. How have you been invincible in your job?
  - Describe one event that seemed so far-fetched, so potentially disastrous that you were sure it would take you down; and you didn't let it.
2. How did that impact your organization?
3. What did you learn about yourself and your ability to make a contribution?
4. How can you transfer that learning to your personal life?

■ ■ ■

No matter what your childhood was like...
No matter what has happened to you...
No matter how many extra pounds you may carry...
No matter what education you never received...
No matter how unworthy you may think you are...
No matter how many gray hairs you may count...
No matter how many times your heart has been broken...
No matter how often you've felt invisible...

You are:

A woman who is powerful...
A woman who is vibrant...
A woman who is trustworthy...
A woman who is beautiful...
A woman who deserves tenderness and love...
A woman whose voice is worthy of being heard...
A woman who makes a difference...
A woman who is invincible.

■ ■ ■

Be Seen

Be Heard

Be Celebrated

Be Yourself

Essay 22

Someday, Someone Is Going to Do Something

Using Your Potential

Potential is a spring-loaded word: The mere mention of it either triggers fear or inspires action; never is it neutral.

Potent—a word that sits right at the beginning of the word potential—references great power, influence, or affect. Add three little letters—"ial"—and, curiously, potential becomes a diluted version of its root. Potential means possibility, capability, latent ability, or capacity. Potent is definitive; potential is passive.

"Potential" speaks of the promise of our life purpose without actually *being* our life purpose. It is the raw goods with which we've been born; and it represents the greatest possibility for our lives. It is the gift before it's unwrapped. It's what we're capable of and what we're built for; but it is not the actual goal we seek.

Like a car without an engine, our potential sits there looking pretty, teasing us with our fantasy of where it can conceivably take us. Without a working engine, however, that car will permanently remain in the driveway. Likewise, our potential remains just another word until we purposefully activate it. Unless we give it our full attention, there is no written guarantee that it will magically turn into something significant. Our potential doesn't come with an owner's manual; it's up to each one of us to uniquely and consciously take the unfettered ingredients of our lives and create a masterpiece with it. Or not.

It's an unfortunate fact that some people with great potential lead uninspired lives, while others with mediocre beginnings maximize every opportunity and lead a life far more exceptional than their lineage would have indicated. Why is that?

> Our potential is the raw goods. Our impact is what we create with it.

Potential in and of itself is *nothing*. Deciding whether to activate our potential is one of the most life-altering choices we'll ever make because either way, there will be an impact. We don't get to carry any unused portion of our potential over into the next lifetime, like we might roll over minutes on our cell phone plan. That's a benevolent way of saying, "You're running out of time—make a choice before there's no choice to make."

"You have so much potential" is usually a euphemism for "You're not living up to your potential" or "If you don't start using some of that potential, you're out of here!" Frequently, we fall in love with someone or something's potential—a new job, a significant other. We're attracted to that *possibility*; not the person or situation as they are in that moment. If the possibility doesn't become reality, we tend to become disappointed, disillusioned, and disheartened.

■ ■ ■

While it is true that our potential is both quantitatively and qualitatively unlimited, it's also inspiring to know that its expiration date doesn't come until the day we die, which means that during our lifetime it is never, ever too late to "turn our *what if* into *what is*." Masses of people lament about some unfulfilled dream, wish, hope, or plan that they've permanently warehoused because they felt they were too old to execute. They had missed the boat, they claimed. So? Take the next one out!

- Too late to take up that hobby? You said that 10 years ago.
- Too old to start your own business? Who said so!
- Too old to return to school and get that sadly missed degree? Not unless you're dead.
- Too old to have a child? Adopt or foster parent.
- Too late for that promotion? Fulfill the requirements now, so you're ready at the next opportunity.
- Too late to write that book? The world needs your experience.
- Too late for love? Never!
- _____
- _____

Dara Torres is the first American swimmer to compete in *five* Olympic Games—over the course of 24 years. She is the oldest member of the Olympic swim team, and is the first woman in history over 40 years of age to swim in the games. She has 12 Olympic medals to her credit, and was 41 when she competed in the 2008 Olympics in Beijing, China. Her last comment before claiming her final medal was this: "You don't have to put an age limit on your dreams." Believe her!

If you *want* your age to be your excuse, then it will be. If you want your gender, financial situation, family, or any other circumstance to be an excuse, it will be. The moment that you decide something is a problem for you, it becomes just that.

What excuses do you use for not getting what you want?

- ☐ I'm afraid I'll fail.
- ☐ People will think I'm stupid to try this.
- ☐ I'm too old.
- ☐ I'm not old enough.
- ☐ There's not enough time.
- ☐ I'm too busy.
- ☐ I don't know how.
- ☐ I don't have the money.
- ☐ My parents expected too little from me.
- ☐ I'm not very good at that.
- ☐ I'll do that as soon as I. . . .
- ☐ I'm lazy.

☐ It doesn't pay enough.

☐ I'm a loser.

☐ Suppose it doesn't work out.

☐ I'm a failure.

☐ I don't get the support I need.

☐ It never occurred to me to ask.

☐ My sister already did that.

☐ No one told me I could.

☐ If I do that, my friends will feel bad.

☐ I'm too fat.

☐ I'm not enough.

☐ It's too hard.

☐ I'm not pretty enough.

☐ Everyone will think I think I'm better than they are.

☐ My fourth grade teacher told me I'd never amount to anything.

☐ My parents expected too much from me.

☐ I don't have a mentor.

☐ I'm afraid.

☐ I'm too much.

☐ I don't have what it takes.

☐ What if no one likes me?

☐ What if everyone likes me?

☐ What if I find out I'm really a horrible person?

☐ It's been done before.

☐ What if it's not what I'm "supposed" to be doing?

☐ I'm scared to let go of what I know.

☐ Suppose it works out and then I'll have to do something else—that's great.

☐ What if I try and I fail?

☐ People will think I'm arrogant.

☐ What if I'm successful and then my friends won't like me?

☐ _____

☐ _____

Note: We're *all* making it up as we go along. We assign meaning through the lens of our experience and beliefs. We can look at our lives as though we failed at something; or we can look at it as if we failed to *do* something. You may want to consider voting for the interpretation that will make you feel best about yourself!

Put a check next to the items that lighten your step and put a smile on your face.

☐ Won't it be great when I succeed at this!

☐ People will admire my courage in doing this.

☐ I'm young enough to go for every dream I have.

☐ Once I have the experience I need, this will be a great next step.
☐ This is the perfect time to experiment with my life.
☐ I'm brainstorming different ways to come up with funds.
☐ I have all the support I need. If I want more, I can ask for it.
☐ This is a real priority for me, so I'm making time for it.
☐ Who am I not to do this?
☐ _____
☐ _____

Having checked these off, what are you thinking and how do you feel right now?

Yes, it is easy to take one look at Dara Torres and make the assertion that she is an exception to every rule; because, quite frankly, she is. But so are you! If you're comparing yourself to anyone right now consider this: They would have one hell of a time and do an indescribably lousy job of being you! Take the effort you're now expending on the "She's better than me" contest and do a happy dance celebrating the fact that you even have the potential: You just can't decide what you want to do with it—yet.

■ ■ ■

The net-net is that the ones who are experimenting with their potential made the decision to set aside their fears (of not being enough, of being alone, of not having the resources, etc.), minimize their limitations, and maximize what they're made of. While you're at it, rethink whether those limitations on your potential are real, or if you're buying into the limitations you've inherited from others.

> Doubt is contagious. So is fear. You can change your friends as easily as you can change your mind.

All of us, at one time in our personal or professional lives, have measured our potential against some unrealized goal. We've then either retreated to a corner, quivering in fear, or jumped into action having used the opportunity to light ourselves up like a Christmas tree.

What happens to the people who don't use their potential? Again, there are two distinct groups: those who recognize that they have potential and choose not to exercise it, and those who don't even bother asking the question. The latter aren't reading this book, so it's immaterial. The former are those who know they have potential but have thus far chosen to allow it to lie dormant. These women have some unusual methods for dismissing themselves. Generally, they will:

- Languish in mediocrity
- Blame others for their failure to succeed
- Develop self-destructive habits as an excuse not to get on with it
- Become depressed
- Daydream about how it will be one day
- Read dozens of self-help books
- Reminisce about how it might have been
- Straighten their desks a lot
- Attend every seminar ever given on "How to Use Your Potential"
- Beat themselves up for not having the courage to show up in their own lives

This "have it but don't use it" group is the very same population that bought $14 billion worth of self-help books last year. I would estimate that about 85 percent of those books were never read; and if they were, the call to action wasn't executed. Do you have a stack of best-selling personal and business development books, most of which have never been read? Join the crowd! Is *Impact!* going to be on top of the pile? I hope not! My assumption is that you're reading this book because you want to live more invincibly and your potential is waiting to be activated. This scenario is making you unhappy, isn't it?

There is nothing that will more quickly render your self-esteem worthless than making yourself a promise that you don't keep— nothing. Every time you buy one of those books—this one included, attend one of those seminars, and swear this time will be different and then it's not, you disappoint yourself and your self-esteem plummets.

Someday is today. Someone is you. Something is your passion.

Conversely, when we accept the challenges we've laid before ourselves; when we keep our promise to ourselves (and, subsequently, to others), our self-esteem noticeably escalates as a reflection of our accomplishments. That's a considerable part of the reason that writing down our goals (and checking them off) so dramatically increases our chances of success. (See Essay #8.)

There's reciprocity between our potential and our self-esteem. It requires a measure of self-esteem to turn your potential into performance. Once you've done that, your self-esteem will in turn rise; which encourages you to turn more of your potential into performance. On the cycle goes, until your life looks and feels much closer to your vision than it once did.

There's an addiction mentality that occurs when we talk about what we're going to do "one day." I recall once observing myself from a distance when I was talking about writing a book. I thought to myself, "I sound like an addict. I'm gonna quit these drugs, yes, I am. This time I really mean it. I'm done with them!" Except that I was *really* saying: "I'm really gonna write that book. Oh, yes, I am. I'm committed this time. This time it's different. This time I really mean it." Cuckoo! (If you've ever been addicted to anything, then you know exactly how I felt.) I think my friends were as embarrassed for me as I was for myself.

Our potential is like window-shopping; we check it out, admire it from afar, envy everyone else's, and wish we could make it ours. Well, we can! We merely have to visit the store when it's *open*; and be willing to pay when we get there.

How do we ignite our potential? How do we turn that temptation into something we can taste? It starts with the conscious choice to do so. The moment we decide that we're ready to take our foot off the brake and convert some of those raw goods into finished products, we send a signal out to the universe: "Red alert. Red alert. She's about to make a move. Everyone—ready yourselves!"

As you clarify your intention and combine it with every iota of focus and personal power within you, the way will begin to open. Your only job at that point will be to take a baby step in the direction you're headed. If you've ever ridden a horse, then you know that the horse will go in the direction you're looking, regardless of what the rest of your body is signaling. The same goes for your life. So look where you're going, see the end from the beginning, and take a step.

---

1. My desire is to: _____

2. By (date): _____

3. I'm afraid that/of: _____

4. The truth is: _____

5. The gifts I have to support this are: _____

6. If I weren't afraid I would: _____

7. What I need to do is this: _____

8. The people who will support me are: _____

9. The first step I need to take is: _____

10. How I will feel when I get it done: _____

We would not be given the potential, vision, or dreams, without also having the gifts and talents to actualize them. In other words, if you've dreamed it, you have every last thing you need to make it happen. Our potential is only the fuel for our life purpose. Our imagination is what's needed to ignite that fuel. When we honor our potential, or stimulate, coax or encourage it, it signals self-respect and self-worth. And you, my friend, deserve it all!

Initiate Impact!

1. Many times you've looked around your organization and had thoughts about all the wonderfully innovative things you could do. Write down one idea for turning that potential into performance.

2. What is the single most significant deterrent to your actualizing your vision?

3. If you're minimizing your ability to create your dreams in your professional life, how is that impacting your vision for your personal life?

Essay 23

I Don't Need Permission! Do I?

Self-Permission

"Permission? You have got to be kidding me. Hello, it's the twenty-first century. I'm an independent woman. I own my own home. I have a spectacular career. I provide exceptionally well for my family. I have all the apparatus that says I've made it. I don't need to ask anyone for anything at any time. And I certainly don't need to ask anyone for permission."

Was I channeling you just then? Are you shaking your head in agreement? Are you scratching your head in confusion?

Great, so let's take a look at this together. Many women bristle at the word "permission" (count me as one of them). For us powerful women, courageous women, successful women, feminist women, or women who have consistently vaulted over the bar we've raised for ourselves, that word noisily announces that we've reverted to the 1950s. Neither a pretty image nor the one we had in mind when we meticulously designed our lives, is it?

We self-sufficient types find the notion of asking for permission to be absurd as well as insulting. Just hearing the word "permission" lands an indignant chip squarely on our shoulders, reminding us that we may still be struggling with the same damn issues we thought our mothers had already handled.

Our language reflects our culture, our beliefs, our social status, our gender, and our age. It reveals who we are. It evolves as we do. Permission has, historically, been just a word. No big deal.

These days? It's spring-loaded! Spoken by a politically incorrect person or one without tact, suggesting women need permission is not just clumsy, but a calamity.

I have personally witnessed any number of usually professional, articulate, brilliant women go up in flames when the words permission and woman were included in the same sentence.

It can trigger our doubts, our fears, and our insecurities. It can remind us that just a few moments ago we were someone's property, we didn't have the right to vote, our existence had to be validated by a man, and that we frequently paid for our freedom with our lives (both literally and figuratively).

■ ■ ■

The past life of permission was other-centered. Survival dictated that women simply had to go "over there" to assume any power which was, at its best, diluted and fleeting. Over there was then, and is still now, patriarchal, in all its manifestations. Forgive the platitude, but until recently women were offered a handout, not a hand up, which kept them in a "one down" position. At its most noble, it looked like charity. At its worst, it was debilitating.

When we contemplate having to ask someone for permission (for food, for shelter, for money, to socialize, to be educated, to be employed, etc.) they are exerting their power *over* us. It broadcasts: They have. We don't. This "other" is in the position to make us do something, which may or may not be against our will. It means our choices have been taken from us or, equally demoralizing, that we had to (or thought we had to) forfeit them—both of which infer that we are incapable of self-determination. In a word, this is hogwash.

Being disempowered by external forces, however, is not the primary concern for women working to rehabilitate their lives and increase their impact. What carves the most enduring ache in our souls is what we do to ourselves, *not* what is done *to* us.

I am not blaming women for this state of affairs: This script was in place well before any of us were even born. What I *am* doing is examining the topic so that you can permanently transform its impact on you; definitely a top priority if your intention is to live invincibly.

> The not so little secret about having to seek permission from someone other than ourselves is that, in order to do so, we have to *abandon* ourselves in the process. That's right. Abandon.

Whenever we go outside of ourselves to get our needs met, (because we have no choice about it, or because we think we have no choice about it), we must leave behind our core Self.

You're probably wondering how that dynamic plays itself out, aren't you? Most of us are fully capable of satisfying our needs ourselves, providing we have the tools and the opportunity. Isn't that so? But here's the dilemma: While we may know that we have the personal power to take ample care of ourselves, we don't always feel as though we have *the right to exercise that power*. The conflict between having the tool but not the permission (from ourselves or someone else) to use it creates unbearable internal tension (and routinely results in learned helplessness). We manage this internal battle by disconnecting from our spirit, our soul, our core Self, thereby minimizing the dissonance. In other words, we blow a fuse and have a personal power outage that disconnects our head from our heart. Yes, it temporarily allows us to function normally but, unfortunately, it does not lead to living happily ever after.

In essence, what the women in prior generations *had* to do, was to pretend (either consciously or not) that they were *less than men*—less smart, less powerful, less capable. All of which required them to stuff their authentic selves into a neat little socially acceptable box and act as though things were hunky-dory. The end result was that women became their own personal perpetrator: What had been done *to* women was now being done *by* women.

For every woman who has ever felt abandoned, whether emotionally, spiritually, or physically, this is the place where it all began. Right in the seat where you're sitting. This is also from where your anger swells. That's where your need to retaliate was born. That's what generates the feelings of not being worthy, not being enough, not being deserving, and not feeling lovable.

> While it's commonly held that most men's biggest fear is emotional engulfment, most women's biggest fear is to be emotionally abandoned. Now you know who's abandoning whom.

■ ■ ■

Let's take this to work, shall we? Note: This scenario is purely for the purpose of providing you with a context for self-permission in the workplace. Obviously generalizations are being made and there is not enough information to accurately assess the situation.

You're sitting in a team meeting with eight of your peers and three senior managers. As Mr. Team Leader goes through the slide deck, you almost give yourself whiplash when you realize that your brainstorm from the last meeting was on two of the slides—with attribution to said gentleman giving the presentation.

You:

A. Say nothing during the meeting but pull the team leader aside later, asking him what he was thinking by taking credit for your genius.

B. Say nothing during the meeting but pull the team leader aside later, asking him if he realized he had made a mistake on the slides.

C. Say nothing and go home at the end of the day thinking, "No big deal, we work together as a team. I'm being a baby about this."

D. Say nothing because the managers were very happy with the outcome of the meeting.

E. None of the above. You didn't even notice that your name wasn't on the slides.

This scenario, like any, depends on the dynamics between the players, the company culture, and a number of other factors. That, of course, is not the point. Assuming that you didn't know whether Mr. Team Leader intentionally took credit where it wasn't due, you had many options, all of which would demonstrate what your level of self-permission and personal empowerment is. What option you chose is secondary to why you chose it.

Both A and B indicate a healthy level of self-permission. Option A, depending on the tone of voice, volume, body language, and so on, might be either aggressive or assertive. Either way, it says that you have good healthy boundaries, that you're unwilling to be taken advantage of, and, by virtue of choosing to speak up rather than let it go, says that you have given yourself permission to be heard, to take care of yourself, to risk confrontation or tension, and to implement your personal power. Well done!

Choosing option B demonstrates self-permission tempered by either politics or nice-girl syndrome. Great that you gave him the benefit of the doubt, but truth be told, if it had been an honest mistake then he would have either said something in the meeting or, immediately after, come to you and acknowledged the error. So the nice-girl act deserves a dose of transparency. You may want to consider what beliefs you have about your right to speak up and defend yourself, your concern about being considered a bitch and, next time, double-checking the slide deck yourself before the meeting.

If you selected option C, it is possible that your level of self-permission has hampered your upward mobility in your organization. Team playing is not to be confused with a lack of integrity. That you were willing to swap them out is indicative of your unwillingness or inability to have a healthy argument with someone. It's likely that you suppress your opinion in many sectors of your life, and that resentment is a feeling you're too intimate with.

There is certainly something to be said for keeping focused on the goal. For those of you who chose option D, let me say this: On the one hand, Bravo. On the other hand, if your colleague did this once, you have a guarantee that he or she will do it again. Next time, however, the ante will be upped. Your level of self-permission is questionable and you may have chosen the path of least resistance. What could you do, right now, to correct the situation and give yourself permission to take up some space?

Lastly, it is likely that if you chose Option E you are either brand new to the team and didn't want to make waves, you had the flu that day and came in anyway, or you were in a support role.

■ ■ ■

There is a minuscule difference between failing to give yourself permission at home and failing to do so at work. Several times throughout this book I referred to women having the desire *"to be seen, heard, and celebrated."* This is a perfect place to expound on that concept.

Women want to be **seen** in all their roles, not just the one you are most familiar with. We are small business owners, wives, girlfriends, daughters, neighbors, C-Suite executives, stay at home moms, etc. Whatever we are doing in our lives, we bring all of those roles with us. When you're in a relationship with us, all of us shows up. We want to know that you know this about us and that you truly see all of us.

We have brilliant ideas, thoughts, opinions, suggestions and the like. When we speak and choose to share some of this with you, we want to know that you **heard** us. We want to know that what we said was received and that it made a difference, an impact.

Although it is lovely fun to be part of a club called 'women', we each consider ourselves quite unique—special, different, rare. We consider ourselves to be one of a kind and we want you to celebrate that in us.

When we allow ourselves to be seen, heard and celebrated, we are giving ourselves permission to be invincible.

Initiate Impact!

1. When you hear the word "permission" what are the first thoughts that come to mind?
2. In what area of your life could you most benefit from some self-permission?
3. How would that change your life and your impact on those around you?
4. Contemplate how you responded to the slide deck scenario. What would you have done? Why?

Essay 24

Permission 2.0

Allowing Yourself to Be Powerful

Permission 2.0 is to women what Web 2.0 is to the high tech industry.

Permission 2.0 represents a paradigm shift in the dynamic between women and their personal power, and how that impacts their ability to live invincibly.

What has evolved, over time and politics, is how we perceive ourselves. Our reality in relation to our power has changed because our perceptions have changed. It is those perceptions that impact our lives and the lives of those with whom we interface. Our perceptions changed because they had to, because it became too darn painful to continue to argue against ourselves.

What does this mean to us? That we can now vote for ourselves instead of voting against the other gender. We can choose to take all the energy that we once spent holding ourselves back, stuffing down our resentment, hiding our anger and allowing ourselves to be victims, and put it to good use: We can use that energy to give ourselves permission.

This 2.0 conversation is about including women in the blueprint for power, not excluding men from the same.

150

This next phase in the evolution of our personal power demands that we own it—fully and full time. Despite our ambivalence about it, we also get to embrace and abide by the responsibility that accompanies personal power (see Essay #10). The times insist that we stop tossing our power "over there" like it's a personal land mine, hoping it will detonate in someone else's life. Did you ever notice that when we do that, we are the ones who suffer the wounds from the shrapnel?

Instead of being resentful of the challenges that go with being powerful, Permission 2.0 encourages us to bring that power as close as we can. Collaborating with it, and with others who have it, will amplify the positive change we create in the world. Call it user participation, if you like. It is a dynamic phenomenon in which we treat permission as a partner crucial to our success and accomplishments: Because it is.

Permission 2.0 does not speak of authority and prerogative, or consent and privilege, nor does it imply that our destiny belongs in the hands of another. Permission 2.0 isn't partnered with someone having power over us, and it has no association with restraint, pain, subjugation, or limitations.

■ ■ ■

Let's take our place, not ask for it.

- If you want to present at the next conference, submit a proposal; don't wait for someone to "discover you."
- If you want the lead on a new project, step up and say so; don't wait for your manager to come knocking.
- If you're not being treated fairly, develop a case and present it; you should always treat yourself better than everyone else does.
- If your manager handed you too many projects that were all due the day before they were given to you, prioritize them with the information you already have—then sit down with him or her

and come up with a strategy that works for both of you; she or he may not have any idea that you were putting in 15-hour days (and won't care unless you care).

- If your best friend has become full maintenance, sit her down and compassionately tell her the truth rather than just walk away because she didn't get it; you'd want someone to do the same for you.
- If your children expect more from you than you're willing to give, set a healthy boundary with them; they are too self-centric to even think about reading your mind.
- If you want to make love tonight, take the initiative with your partner; don't expect him or her to guess that tonight's the lucky night.

Permission 2.0 is all about us. It is we who grant ourselves authorization to do whatever we want. It is we who have license to stamp approval on our plans for our purpose. It is we who gives ourselves life's green light.

This is a radically different life than our mothers and grandmothers chose for themselves: It's a whole new game we're now playing. We get to make up our own rules as we go along—rules custom designed to fit idiosyncratic us.

■ ■ ■

Permission 2.0 is to your success what gas is to your car. Without it, you're not going anywhere.

The word permission comes from the Latin verb, permittere, which means *allow*. It's not the meaning of the word that has changed over time, but the interpretation of the meaning that has been transformed. In our culture, "allowing" once meant that something was extended from one person to another. Perhaps the first idea we need to get used to is that no one is going to save us. The second idea is that we don't need saving. We have power to spare. What I know to be true, in the context of women's self-empowerment, is that we are both the giver and the receiver of permission. It is we who give ourselves permission. Or not.

> It is synonymous with *allowing*. You may not have to put your foot on the accelerator; you just need to take it off the brake.

What is it that you want? Where would you like to grant yourself permission? If there were no one in the world whose judgments would interfere with life's enticements, what would be on the top of your "get to give yourself" list?

Would it be

☐ permission to be the leader?
☐ permission to leave that 20-year relationship?
☐ permission to leave old friends behind?
☐ permission to speak your mind?
☐ permission to disagree with your boss's boss's boss?
☐ permission to follow instead of lead?
☐ permission to stop being a victim?
☐ permission to go for that job that you're not totally qualified for?
☐ permission to ask for a raise when there's no money in the budget?
☐ permission to return to school for a degree you've always wanted?
☐ permission to get married at 50 years old?
☐ permission to not have any children?
☐ permission to put something down, like guilt or envy?
☐ permission to walk away from that mediocre job?
☐ permission to be a stay-at-home mom?
☐ permission to tell the truth?
☐ permission to forgive?

☐ permission to not apologize?
☐ permission to not go for it now?
☐ permission to stay single?
☐ _____
☐ _____
☐ _____
☐ _____

■ ■ ■

When I first coined the term Permission 2.0 in 2004, I was looked at rather oddly, and I was frequently asked to repeat myself (neither of which is actually rare). Reminiscent of the 1950s, the notion of permission still carried with it the stigma of political incorrectness. I found that people either denied its role in their success or treated the word like toxic waste. When I toyed with the idea, however, of naming this book Permission 2.0, 100 percent of my focus group said that people wouldn't get it; that it would trigger the "I give you permission" button in the reader. I think we sell one another short.

The current incarnation of "permission" was born out of, and is anchored to, the notion that we arrived on our birth day equipped with everything we need to live our life purpose and to have maximum impact. What is required of us to live invincibly is that we:

◆ Make room for something that already exists
◆ Give it permission to express itself
◆ Provide it with an environment in which it can flourish

In a sentence: Permission 2.0 is an invitation to *get out of the way* of our dreams, aspirations, and desires, and to *stop interrupting our own success*.

You know what that sounds like: "But, but, but. . . ." Please, ladies, let's put those buts behind us, where they belong.

It seemed revolutionary when I first realized that if we want to turn our potential into performance, we don't have to do anything; we have to stop doing some things. Think about it—we already have everything we need to be successful. We just have to sit still and take a comprehensive inventory of what we already have. We are already the person we strive to be. We don't have to do one more thing to become more of, or better at, who we already are. We can *relax*. Our only job is to show up as authentically, as truthfully, as transparently, and as congruently as humanly possible.

Here's the real beauty of the thing: *It's our choice alone,* and there are few places in life where we can honestly claim that. The decision to be ourselves and to both risk the vulnerability that comes with it, and reap the infinite rewards as a result of having done so, is entirely up to us. No one else gets to weigh in on the decision. There's no committee, no consensus, no vote but our own. How liberating is that!

All that time we spent improving ourselves, saving ourselves, and changing ourselves could have been better spent just *being* ourselves. All that energy could have been put toward becoming the woman we want to grow into. To think of the tens of thousands of dollars we've spent on therapy getting to that very basic conclusion: That we were okay to start with and then the world around us wanted us to change. Now that we're some distance down the road, we can take what we learned from the fallout and turn it into something usable for our future, for who we are planning to become when we give ourselves even more permission 2.0.

Permission 2.0 has nothing to do with becoming someone we're not, and everything to do with being more of who we already are.

Permission 2.0 extends to who we want to become, going forward: Who we've decided we deserve to evolve into over time. We don't get where we're going by staying fabulous forever: Inevitably we'll have to get confused again if we're to grow into a bigger, more invincible version of ourselves.

For the present, we don't have to lose that five pounds in order to be acceptable. We don't have to know how to talk to him in bed in order to be considered a desirable woman. We don't need to get flat abs in 10 days or learn the five secrets to anything in order to lead a powerful life. Phew! Now isn't that's a relief? This also means that we don't have to feel compelled to compare ourselves to the airbrushed teenagers on the covers of the women's magazines at the checkout stands, either. Collective sigh.

All of which sets the stage for us to become as strategic about what we want for our lives as we are about what we want for our businesses. A long-range plan is not two days, it is 3 or 5 years. A long-term strategy doesn't just come to us, we have to plan for it.

The Permission 2.0 Challenge is a template for such a plan. Go to my website, www.frominvisibletoinvincible.com and download your free copy. Make it your own!

Initiate Impact!

1. Where in your life would giving yourself permission enable you to live more invincibly and have more impact?
2. Where will you give yourself permission to make a greater contribution at work?
3. In what ways would your relationships be enhanced if you gave yourself permission to love more freely?
4. What should you be asking for (or taking) that you're waiting for? (Examples: lead on a project, setting boundary with kids.)

Essay 25

Thoughtus Interruptus
Don't Believe Everything You Think

I'm going to tell you a secret that is going to change the way you look at your psychological health—and the way you perceive all those crazy yet wonderful people whom you call family. But before I do that, I want to share a little story.

Have you ever had a conversation that left you wanting to take a shower afterward? This anecdote did that for me. Several years ago I facilitated a *Women, Courage, Leadership, conference* in my hometown. The day following this successful event, I touched base with a senior HR person from one of the local corporations who had participated. Toward the end of our conversation, she made a remark that I hope I will always remember. Pam said, "But you and I, Nancy, both know that we would have preferred a higher caliber woman at the event." We then wrapped up our conversation and she, I assume, moved on with the rest of her day. I, on the other hand, needed to sort out why I had the willies.

I replayed our conversation several times before I got to the root of what had so offended me. The words Pam chose implied that she would have preferred more senior executives and fewer entry level women in attendance: But it was her condescension, and the insinuation that women who are beginning their careers are somehow less than or not as good as their senior counterparts that set me on my heels. Pam assumed that more experienced and senior women have different issues than their junior counterparts. Not!

This is where the not-so-secret secret about your psychological health comes in. By my tally, I had probably worked with several thousand people by the time I met Pam. If I'd learned nothing else, I'd learned that no matter who they were; no matter what level of accomplishment they had achieved; regardless of their age, ethnicity, religion, or sexual preference—there are only *four essential core wounds* from which one suffers. In other words, when you open that baggage of yours, every item you unpack will fit into one of these four categories of issues. The emotional playing field is, in practice, a leveled one!

> Irrespective of whether you are the CEO of a multibillion dollar conglomerate, a small business owner, an entry level administrative assistant, or a stay-at-home mom—your issues are identical.

The only variable is that a senior executive is going to have a greater *amount* of risk than will a junior assistant; she will have greater fiduciary responsibilities and the number of people who rely on her will be greater. All other factors remain the same. While a new manager might be responsible for five employees, a senior vice president might be responsible for five hundred. While a mid-level manager might have a seven-figure budget, an executive vice president might have a nine-figure one: the degree of people's risk, of course, is commensurate with their experience.

During your lifetime you will be faced with some or all of these same issues, each with a varying degree of impact on you. You will have a primary wound that you've dealt with for most of your life and you'll have had at least one dance with the other three. The only 'aha' might be that you didn't realize you weren't alone; that this wounding is 'normal' and, in fact, instrumental in your psychosocial development. So, relax—there is nothing 'wrong' with you.

Perhaps you're wondering what those four essential core wounds
are? In no particular order:

  ◆ I'm not worthy
  ◆ I don't deserve
  ◆ I'm not enough
  ◆ I'm not lovable

Although these should be relatively self-explanatory, I'll make a
few clarifying points. The terms *deserve* and *worthy* are usually synonymous; the distinction here is that "deserve" is an external qualifier,
while "worthy" is an internal qualifier. When someone experiences not
deserving, it usually means something material, as in, "I don't deserve
to make as much money as I'd like;" or "I don't deserve that promotion." In contrast, when someone experiences not worthy, it generally
means something internal, such as, "I'm not worthy of love," or "I'm
not worthy of respect."

Feelings of "I'm not enough" show up in many different forms:
"I'm not smart enough." "I'm not pretty enough." "I'm not experienced
enough." This 'enoughness' results from the outside world perpetually
reminding women that if we just do something more, better, or different,
we will finally be okay .

All four of these core wounds have equal impact on a woman's
self-esteem; none is worse than the other and none of them are easy
to live with. All of them can be worked through, healed, resolved,
and reversed, but *not* completely. Although our core wounds never
vanish, we *can* expect that as the underlying issues are addressed,
their impact will fade. Instead of occupying most of your emotional
peripheral vision, they'll crop up less and less; until, at some point,
you'll forget you even have the issues—except on occasions when
something triggers them. What can you do? Increase your awareness of
how these issues show up in your life; work to resolve them; shrink
their impact on you; and look where you're going.

> What makes these core wounds a *splendid gift* is what you can learn to do with them: Make no mistake—healing is a learned process.

Nothing changes when you rely on magic, fairy dust, or hope. Just be truthful about what's not working for you and do whatever it takes to clear it from your life. You can do this!! You've done it before.

Of course, you always have the option to pick up where whoever helped you to create these wounds left off, and become your own worst enemy by perpetuating the very circumstances that created this hurt in the first place. Someone who was raised with emotional abuse and repeatedly heard about how worthless, stupid, and so on she was—and continues throughout her adulthood to talk to herself in the same manner—is an example of this. She's engaging in behavior that's familiar, and that has become a habit. It is learned behavior, which means it can be unlearned, given enough motivation. This is a cause for celebration! It is in your control. It is your choice.

> A more powerful choice, however, would be to use this wound as a magnificent, efficient, and powerful tool in your journey to become invincible.

How can you do that? It's actually easy, given the alternative (living with it for the rest of your life). Without intervention, our behavior is a perfect expression of our wounds; our actions unambiguously tell the world what our supposedly invisible agenda is. Those with meager self-awareness might just as well march through town wearing a sandwich board posting their wounds. So if you think that no one knows what your "stuff" is, think again!

Our actions are a product of our thinking, aren't they? When we're trotting about in our lives with an unexamined or open wound, our behavior both *demonstrates* and *proves* our wound. The difference between the two is simple to understand. When we set out to *prove* anything, our behavior emanates from our ego, which means fear is involved. In essence, we're going to prove to the world, tough gals that we are, that we're not messed up; which ultimately serves only to show the world exactly how messed up we truly are.

When we set out to *demonstrate* anything, our behavior emanates from our heart, from our divine self, and from love. We know who we are, we're confident of our value, and we're going to unselfishly give of who we are simply because we're so grateful for the gifts we've been given. This will all make perfect sense to you when you see this theory applied in Katrina's story.

I'd like to introduce you to Katrina, an upper-level manager in the telecommunications industry. Katrina is in her early forties, married to a stay-at-home husband for a dozen years, with two elementary school children. She's absolutely beautiful inside and out, and has been adored by the management who progressed her rapidly in her career.

When she was entering puberty, Katrina's father had an affair and, subsequently, married his paramour. He literally left her family overnight. Katrina felt hopelessly abandoned, and her mother reinforced to her that her dad had no concern for her well-being. As he was out of communication for several years, Katrina didn't have any input to the contrary, and believed that she had been abandoned. When she was in her early thirties she connected with her father in such a way that she could ask him for his version of what had happened. Predictably, it was quite different from what she'd been told: He claimed that her mother refused to let him see her and her brother.

Fast forward to today. When I met Katrina she had no idea that this 20-year-old event was still monopolizing her psyche. She was carrying an extra 40 pounds, and her husband wasn't communicating with her—she was afraid they'd end up in divorce court. She was troubled by her feelings of diminished worth, and no number of promotions or salary increases registered success for her. What Katrina discovered was that her dad's departure had left her feeling not only abandoned, but unlovable and unworthy.

Like many women who feel unworthy, Katrina was a doormat (see Essay #13). Her own actions allowed others to treat her as such, and she was scarcely aware that this dynamic was even playing itself out in her life. She worked constantly: at her job, at others' jobs, at her marriage, at motherhood, at everything other than taking care of herself. Sound familiar? Yes, I think all women have, at some point in their lives, thought, "The more I do, the greater the chance someone will _____". As you probably know by now, this doesn't work.

The more Katrina worked at keeping her life together, the more it fell apart. The cleaner she made her home, the less her husband helped out. The more money she made, the more he spent. The more she worked at her job, the more was expected of her. Katrina spent every minute of every day trying to prove that she was worthy and lovable. She felt that if she just did one more thing for her husband, then he would never leave her. If she just did one more extra project at work then they would never fire her (read: abandon). Katrina's attempts to *prove* her self-worth and lovability exhausted her to the point where she no longer recognized who she was, or that she had a choice about her lifestyle.

By the time she came to me for coaching she was frayed at the edges and was scared silly about where her mental health was headed. Like all of us, Katrina was doing the best she knew how. Having spent decades in this gerbil-like pattern, it never even occurred to Katrina that she could have simply demonstrated who she was by authentically showing up in her life, imperfections and all; giving others the chance to see the beauty and truth that radiates from her.

A few weeks into our work together, I gave Katrina the assignment to track her decision-making process for two days. Since her issues revolved around her self-worth, that became her focus. I don't know how many decisions we make every day, but it must be thousands; big ones such as, "Do I accept that job offer?" to little ones like, "Which side of the bed do I get out of in the morning?" My request was that Katrina document as many decisions as she possibly could.

Decision	To Prove "I'm Worthy"	To Prove "I'm Not Worthy"	To Demonstrate My Personal Power

FIGURE 25.1   To Prove vs. to Demonstrate Chart

Every single choice of every single day is decided (whether consciously or not) from one of three vantage points:

To prove that you are_____.

To prove that you are *not*_____

To demonstrate your personal power, and therefore, your invincibility.

What Katrina discovered from doing this exercise was that eighty percent of her decisions came from her unconscious attempts to prove that she was worthy; having sex when she didn't feel like it (worthy to be a wife), taking on extra work for which she had no time (worthy to be an executive), taking her children to the park when what she really needed was a nap (worthy to be a mother). Fifteen percent of her decisions—carrying extra weight, not getting enough sleep, and staying too late at the office—were made in her attempt to prove that she wasn't, after all, worthy. A meager 5 out of every 100 decisions she made were from the place of "I am powerful. I am invincible. I am Katrina, and I am proud of that!"

Now, you may be thinking to yourself: "Gee, that woman is sure neurotic." But I can assure you that she is no more neurotic than many of us. She didn't carry a banner that said, "I'm not worthy." She was just "a little down," "exhausted," "not appreciated," and felt as though she was "working way too hard to be happy." "I don't feel like myself—but I no longer know what 'myself' feels like."

Katrina reported that this exercise literally changed her life. Why? We can't move from Point A (our wound) to Point B (our healing/personal power) until we have an accurate assessment of where Point A *is*. Most of us are so sublimely unconscious about our motivations and what inspires us to do what we do that we literally walk blindly through our lives and use the catchphrase "I don't know" instead of "I'll find out." Katrina, too, had absolutely no idea as to what the force was behind her decisions. Although she hadn't been happy, she was shocked to learn of the extent to which this event from her adolescence ruled her entire life and influenced almost all of her behavior. For the first time in many years, she now has choices; choices are the equivalent of freedom, personal power, and what will lead to our invincibility.

Few exercises are as singularly powerful as the one in Figure 25.1. I implore you to do this exercise in your own life, using one of the four essential core wounds at a time (I don't deserve, I'm not worthy, I'm not enough, I'm not lovable). I give you my word that it will be worth the effort.

Our actions stems from our thoughts. If we don't like what we're experiencing in our lives, then we must *think about what we think*. We must implement Thoughtus Interruptus! Katrina was so preoccupied with her old habits that it never dawned on her to stop and examine the correlation between what she was thinking (I'm not worthy) and how she was feeling and behaving (worthless).

If you don't like how you're feeling, then change what you're thinking. If you don't believe me, try this yourself. Think about some unhappy event that happened in your life. How do you feel? Now think about some joyous occasion. Now how do you feel? What's the point? We're at choice about how we feel. We're at choice, in every moment, to interrupt what we're thinking (because we don't like how that thought is making us feel), and select a different thought which corresponds to the feeling we desire.

Our thoughts are just that: our thoughts. They have nothing to do with objective truth. Actually, there is no such thing as objective truth, only subjective truth. Given that, if you want to feel powerful, happy, joyous, and successful then

"Don't believe everything you think."

You choose what you think. You choose your focus. You choose your perspective. You choose your attitude. You choose courage. You choose to be powerful. You choose to be on purpose. You choose your path. *Or the world chooses for you.* P.S. Failing to choose may, indeed, imply choosing to fail.

*A woman goes to the doctor and says, "Every time I bang
my head with my hand, my head hurts." The doctor replies,
"Then stop doing it!"*

Initiate Impact!

1. Which of the four essential core wounds do you most identify with?
2. Do the exercise shown in Figure 25.1—the same one Katrina did—substituting your primary essential core wound. Track as many decisions as you possibly can in a 48-hour period.
3. What did you learn?
4. How will you change what you're thinking and doing as a result of this discovery?
5. What are the thoughts that you have about your business that might be standing in the way of you producing the results you desire?

Essay 26

Self of Steam
Self-Esteem and Impact

On a sunny Saturday afternoon, I took my family out for a drive. There was nothing unusual about that save the fact that I'd not remembered my mini digital tape recorder. It had become my constant companion since I'd begun writing; as I went through my day, I'd record the thought nuggets that would be transformed into chapters by night's end.

I asked my daughter, Lily, to find something to write with and jot down some ideas I had. At the end of our little road trip, I asked her for the sheet of paper, thinking that I'd spend an hour or two at my computer. As I skimmed the list I commented to myself that she'd done a great job writing down exactly what I'd asked her to. She's sophisticated, smart in her heart, and a great student, this little one of mine. Then I reached item number seven on the list. It read "self of steam."

Me: Honey, what's this self-of-steam? (giggling to myself)
Lily: You told me to write that down.
Me: Could it have been "self-esteem"?
Lily: Noooooo. You *said* self-of-steam!
Me: I never realized how close the two sounded.
Lily: *You told me self-of-steam!*
Me: (Giggle gone—completely wiped out by her tone of voice. I had momentarily forgotten that 11-year-olds know everything.) Would you like me to explain what self-esteem means?

Lily: I know what it means. I have a lot of it. Everyone at school tells me so. All the teachers say that I'm very powerful, that I speak my mind, and that no one can bully me.

Me: Okay then. Yes, sweetheart. You do, indeed, have a self-of-steam!

And she does. This little girl has more confidence, more self-assurance, more poise, and a stronger sense of self than most women quadruple her age. She was born that way. I've also worked diligently to cultivate it in her; which I might add, has been both supremely rewarding and remarkably challenging at the same time. Lily knows no fear, cannot be intimidated, can argue you out of your own shoes, and has the end-of-the-day effect of making me feel as though I've been nibbled to death by a thousand minnows. Now if we could only bottle that self-of-steam....

My mother, once again, was right. "Wait until you have children!" she repeatedly told me. I'm laughing as I confess that Lily couldn't be more of a mirror for me, reflecting back my willfulness, my tenaciousness, my blind spots—all of it! The irony? She's adopted! There's no crediting the gene pool for our similarities; and, yes, self-esteem is, to a large degree, influenced by our biology.

■ ■ ■

Our self-esteem is, in the simplest of terms, our opinion of ourselves. It represents how much (or little) we value ourselves and how well we perceive ourselves. Included in this calculation is the estimation of how important we think we are, as well as our level of self-worth; how we feel about who we are and about our accomplishments.

It should be emphasized that this book is not the appropriate venue for deep psychological work, or for the assessment and diagnosis of your mental health: It is not a substitute for counseling or therapy. I'm introducing the topic of self-esteem because it is fundamental for your personal and professional success. A straight line can easily be drawn between our self-esteem and our self-confidence—which is a key component to life success. Self-confidence leads to self-trust and healthy risk taking, which in turn begets innovative thinking and creative problem solving. And voilà—you have impact!

> If you are waiting for the day when you haven't any personal is-
> sues; when you have worked through all your childhood wounds;
> when your up never has a down; when you are "done" with in-
> trospection; and when you are, finally, self-aware—then wait no
> more!

That day does not exist until you reach your expiration date; and at
that point, you won't care. Everyone has baggage. Your only job is to
know what's in yours.

This is a tease of my "normal" daily schedule:

9:00	client's parents loved her too much
10:00	client's parents didn't love her enough
11:00	client's parents abandoned her
12:00	client's parents stifled her
1:00	client had too much responsibility
2:00	client had no responsibility
3:00	child had no emotional support
4:00	child had too much emotional support.

Everyone has something to deal with. In this respect, emotional
issues are an equal opportunity employer. In fact, I can already hear
my daughter in *her* first therapy session.

Lily: Do you have any idea how hard it was to grow up with a mother
who totally believed in me? Who always supported me? Who told
me I could do whatever I set my mind to? Do you know the pressure of being treated powerfully all of your childhood, of learning
to make your own decisions, and of earning consequences instead
of punishment?

I hope I'm still laughing when this happens. There is only one thing
we can do about our childhood, no matter what it looked like or felt

like: appropriately adjust our perception of it in the present, in the now. That's it. We can't go back in time and change any of the details, but we most certainly can change how we view those formative years.

> Everyone arrives on earth with a laundry list of issues that they get to work through this lifetime. The person who doesn't have a laundry list lives only in one place—the movies.

Got that?

So the transformative question is: Which laundry list would you have preferred to have signed up for? I have personally seen a zillion of them, and I can assure you that given the choice between your list and someone else's, you will always pick your own. Why? Because those issues that cause you the most strife, that keep you tossing and turning at night, that chew away at your self-esteem, and inflate your feelings of worthiness are the perfect tools to get you to your life purpose: They are your life insurance policy guaranteeing that you will have impact and that you are, indeed, invincible!

Initiate Impact!

1. What emotional issues have kept you company most of your life?
   - How do they impact your life?
   - How do these issues impact your work?
2. Which family members deal with the same issues?
3. What's one thing you can do today to take a step to heal and diminish the impact of that issue on your life?

Essay 27

There's No 'We' In Courage

Living Courageously

"Does anyone want to go to the bathroom with me?" This is the woman's chant heard round the country, from ball games to ballrooms. We women have a proclivity to herd—think sheep—and are loath to do much of anything without our entourage close beside us. It's like mobile group therapy.

Most of us seek out and ultimately thrive on consensus around all of our decisions. Prior to making any major move in our lives (and smaller ones as well), we check in with our friends; we rehash the details; we cover the concerns; we weigh the options; and we basically talk it to death. Once we have performed a complete autopsy on the issue, we can then be certain that we're ready to make that courageous move. "Get off the horse, it's dead."

We shop, we eat, we work, we play, we exercise—with other women. Why? Because it's more fun that way! Think of it as a lifestyle choice.

> Our only resistance to courage is that it's not
> a team sport.

Here's where we're apt to hold ourselves back: When we choose to be courageous we are also, unwittingly, choosing to be alone. For

171

most women, there are few circumstances less desirable than being sequestered with our own thoughts, and having to trust ourselves without the benefit of polling our colleagues. We are physiologically and sociologically programmed for relationship, which is why so many of us opt out or ignore splendid opportunities, especially at work; our tolerance for risk erodes in proportion to how much we're required to trust ourselves (see Essay #28).

As we accrue life experience, courageous women come to accept that we alone generate the power that creates the results in our lives; that as much fun as it is to travel in troops and commiserate in committees, the truth about courage is that it's a crazy cocktail consisting of *our* values, *our* intentions and *our* impact. Ours alone; no we in sight.

It takes a lot of chutzpah to live courageously. When we whittle away all the rhetoric, to be courageous simply means to live life for and from ourselves. When we show up authentically in our lives it is *the* extreme gesture of self-trust and gratitude. It declares that we are living our lives according to our inner compass, our internal GPS (God Positioning System). It means we follow our own guidance in every word, thought, and deed regardless of what the outside world is demanding of us or relying on us to provide.

> There is a very fine line between courage and stupidity, and there will be many times when even the most powerful woman won't be confident of which side of that line she is standing on.

This line is easily blurred or confused when we're not certain of the place from which we make our decisions: From the heart, where love lives, or from the ego, where fear resides. All choices—regardless of size—are generated from one of these two places. The option we select depends upon our history, its imprint on our present, and its implication for our future. Every choice is a new one; without choice, there is no courage.

Stupid choices are the ones we make without stopping to check in with ourselves to see if there's congruency between our heart and our head; and learning that there isn't when it's too late to do anything about it. Those are the decisions we make when we're on autopilot, when we ignore our inner wisdom, our voice of intuition, and when we think someone else's opinion is our own. Foolish choices are usually made when we unconsciously default to our tried and true family of origin issues. In our attempts to prove something to them—that we're powerful, successful, intelligent, savvy, and so on—we end up doing the opposite (see Essay #25).

Every opportunity is a learning opportunity; we don't make mistakes or get it wrong if we manage to learn something from it. So when I cheekily refer to 'stupid' choices, I don't actually mean that we're unintelligent. I mean that these decisions spring from our ego and are based on *fear*; they do not come from our purpose, they're unrelated to courage, and they do not leave favorable impact. Like these:

- ◆ Sue applied for a job to 'prove' that she's as smart as her sister
- ◆ Joe bought a house beyond his means to prove to his friends that he's successful
- ◆ Mark went to law school only because his dad did, and he wanted his dad to love him more

The *courageous* counterpart to these decisions would be:

- ◆ After discovering her life purpose, Sue found the ideal job for herself; she excelled and went on to write her own ticket
- ◆ Joe analyzed his financial goals and determined how much house he could afford. It wasn't the biggest on the block, but it will be paid for in fifteen years
- ◆ Mark earned his MBA; he'd always pictured himself as a serial entrepreneur

The more courageously we live, the greater the risk that we will err on the side of being human. We will, at many junctures, make mistakes while trying to prove that we are worthy, deserving, lovable or enough. Regardless of whether we're courageous or sissies, on purpose or off, in our hearts or in our heads—we will alternately jump rope with both courageous and stupid decisions. Despite what we might think we know, human nature craves the contrast these two places provide.

■ ■ ■

Being courageous might involve the decision to do something, the decision not to do something, or the decision to merely stand still. While we could say the same of stupidity there is one major difference here.

> When we are courageous we are authentic and present. When we are stupid we pretend we are someone else.

The dictionary defines the word "authentic" as synonymous with "legitimate." This, by deduction, implies that anything else is illegitimate—something I know to be completely true.

We all know people who perceive that they have some fatal flaw or imperfection that must remain hidden from all who meet them. The shame and humiliation that has accumulated around this so-called deficiency has made them appear to be someone they're not. Similarly, I have encountered women who are so lacquered in self-hatred that they are only willing to show the world the "good stuff"—the qualities for which they would most be admired. In both cases, these people are more committed to looking good than feeling good; and they're short on the mettle for courage.

It takes an extraordinary amount of self-awareness, self-esteem, confidence, and commitment to show the world who we are at our core; to drop the masks, leave the wiles to the wayside, and relinquish pretense and posturing.

Think about it for a minute. Consider how much grit it takes to put your life in full view of everyone you care about and respect, and make decisions independent of their influence and despite their opinions. The more you care about them, the harder this will be. Courage means that while you may consider the thoughts and feelings of those who you respect, at the end of the day, it is only your voice that registers a sound.

Did I mention that sometimes being courageous is no fun at all?

> Just because it's the right thing to do doesn't
> mean that it's the easy thing to do.

Courageous decisions are not by any means uncomplicated or easy decisions. They are seldom clear and direct, or precise and organized, and they can create a surplus of cognitive dissonance (a fancy phrase for inner turmoil). Courageous decisions can be extraordinarily painful to make and to live with. They come without guarantees; and we'll never know what would have happened had we made some other choice, will we? But that's what makes them ours and that's what makes them courageous. That's why courage is worth talking about; it makes us vulnerable, and is rare and priceless.

- ◆ Just because our decision is courageous does not mean that we will celebrate it.
- ◆ Just because our decision is courageous does not mean that we'll be 100 percent excited about it.
- ◆ Just because our decision is courageous does not mean that we will be without our doubts about it.
- ◆ Just because our decision is courageous does not mean that it will be without conflict.
- ◆ Just because our decision is courageous does not mean that we will walk away and live happily ever after.
- ◆ Just because our decision is courageous does not mean that our mothers will approve of us, or that our fathers will be proud of us.

If you live your life looking only for safety, you will wake up one day standing on the wrong side of the courage-stupidity line, wondering what on earth happened.

> The only safety that exists is in knowing that you can trust yourself to make a great choice regardless of life circumstances.

"Safety is an illusion; courage is its antidote."

Initiate Impact!

1. Reflect back to a few of the most courageous things you've ever done in your life.
    - Maybe ended a relationship with someone you loved because you knew in your heart that it wasn't good for you?
    - Maybe taken a job, purely on speculation, because your gut told you it was the right move?
    - Maybe you turned down a client knowing it was just not a good fit no matter what anyone said?
2. What were the circumstances?
3. What made you trust yourself?
4. What made this an act of courage?
5. What was the worst thing that could have happened?
6. How did that measure against the upside?

Essay 28

OMG! My Eggs Are Stale!

Self-Trust

Much attention is paid to my having adopted two newborns as a single parent. True, it does make me more out of the ordinary than not; but so do a number of other things about me. So, why this one? Regardless of whether I'm in a media interview, on the speaking circuit, or among new friends—the automatic response to this tidbit about me is always the same: "Wow! You did that on your own? You are so courageous!" My response? "Courageous? Adopting my babies had nothing to do with courage. It was love and desire that compelled me." Interesting how our lives appear to others, isn't it?

Why do people automatically assume that my decision was courageous? Probably because they recognize that it involved a humongous helping of self-trust—a commodity that we *all* fear we're lacking. This decision of mine was so much simpler than you might think. Simple; not *easy*. Some self-disclosure here, between you and me? I wanted to be a mommy. I was single. My eggs were stale. So I adopted. Okay, maybe it wasn't quite that simple; but given the alternative—being childless—it was both an obvious and straightforward choice for me.

■ ■ ■

Prior to deciding to adopt, I'd walked the beach for over a year trying to figure out how to become a mommy. First I opted for the donor insemination route: During the process the nurse spilled the sperm down my leg (nobody makes up this stuff!). Next I tried the "friends with benefits" route. Let's just say I'd never recommend it. One morning while driving to the supermarket, I asked God out loud for guidance (hey, you pray your way, I'll pray mine). "Just give me a clear sign as to how I can become a mommy." Following a bit of begging and groveling (still out loud, always with God) I began to ponder my rapidly approaching fortieth birthday. I found myself calculating the probability of meeting a fantastic man, falling madly in love, and getting pregnant before the end of the month. It didn't look good. Minutes later, at the next stop light, I pulled up behind a car whose license frame said, "Adopt a Child. Call 800.xxx.xxxx)." I swear.

Did I get the message? No! I can be quite the stubborn one. Five more months went by before I opened myself to the possibility of adoption. In the end it came down to one more menstrual cycle I was hoping not to have, a dinner with a new friend who was just venturing into adoption agency territory, and a number of messages from my inner wisdom that I simply couldn't miss. Three months later, I headed for Cambodia to bring my daughter home.

What did I learn? Self-trust. Not what it was; but that I indeed had it. That despite my circumstances, or maybe because of them; that regardless of the influx of commentary from those who love me and respect me; that irrespective of what others say is normal or acceptable or expected; we all must figure out and do what is right for us. These are lonely choices we make.

> Nobody—and I mean nobody—gets to weigh in on these kinds of life-changing decisions; because, at the very end of the day, we are the only ones who have to live with them—for the rest of our lives.

■ ■ ■

Trust of self...hmm. Why is this not easy for us? I find it curious that we trust the opinion of complete strangers, our dysfunctional culture, colleagues we've known for only three months, the media, and our wacky and wonderful relatives—all more than we trust the one person who we've known our entire lives—*ourselves*. How crazy is that? And why do we do that? Especially when you consider that the times we most regret are those when we didn't listen to our inner wisdom; when we thought others knew what was better for us than we knew for ourselves; and when we were vetoed by those who knew us best and loved us most. To be short on self-trust makes no logical sense at all, if we stop and think about it.

> Like intuition, self-trust is a muscle; if we don't consistently use it over time, it atrophies. Conversely, the more we exercise it, the stronger, more enduring, and resilient it becomes.

I wonder if we trust an outsider more than our insider so that we don't have to be responsible for an unfavorable outcome; so that if "it" doesn't work out, we have someone to blame besides the person in the mirror. Unquestionably there are many women with colossal accountability issues (it's a problem for men, as well, but the issue looks different for them). Our diminished level of self-trust is tied to our issues around accountability (see Essay #21—it's devoted entirely to the subject) as well as the way most of us have been socialized.

For hundreds of years, women have been in the "one-down" position where they had no choices, made few decisions, and relied on others (namely their husbands, family, and society) to tell them who and how to be, what to do, and how to do it. Not exactly a fertile breeding ground for the cultivation of self-trust, is it?

If we step inside ourselves for a moment, we'll remember a basic truth. We'll recall the times when our intuition served us exceedingly well and those other times when—although we may have *wanted* to— we did not heed it; and we paid a dear price for the net result as well as for ignoring ourselves. If our intuition is as reliable as it's reputed to be, then shouldn't our degree of self-trust match it? And if it doesn't, why not?

Is it that we can't trust ourselves, or that we're unwilling to confirm just how trustworthy we are? You may be asking yourself why women would avoid *knowing* they're trustworthy while taking comfort in *believing* they are.

> Believing is laced with hope; knowing is
> believing without the doubt; and nothing
> good comes out of doubt.

The second we hope something will happen, we are indicating a lack of self-trust. The implicit message behind hope is that the power to actualize whatever it is we're hoping for lies outside ourselves; over there somewhere. When we say we know something, we are certain of it, and no hope is necessary because we own it as the truth. When we know the things we know, it is reliable to the same degree of certainty that we will be the same gender when we wake up in the morning as when we went to bed. There's no reason even to check, is there?

> The minute a woman says, "I'm not sure," she is.

Almost without exception when a woman says to me, "I'm not sure about . . ." and I question her, press her to decide whether she is certain of what she's saying, she usually is. Why, then, the hesitation? Why the unwillingness to commit to knowing something? To trusting oneself?

It's a way we hedge, or manipulate language to cover our tushes. God forbid we say anything too brazen, too self-assured, too absolute, too smart, too bossy or too powerful. "I'm not sure" is also a way for women to prostrate themselves: We can appear to be collaborative, relational and agreeable, even when we don't care to be. (The whole subject of women being "too" is addressed in Essay #15.)

Do you find this illogical? I do! And if you think reading about it is wringing the energy out of you, you might start tracking the havoc this creates in your life and on your psyche; to say nothing of what it does to your ability to have impact.

> Self-trust is vital for self-permission.
> Self-permission is vital for self-empowerment.
> Self-empowerment is the only road that leads to impact.

■ ■ ■

The extent to which we trust others before ourselves is the extent to which we disempower ourselves. What does it take to trust ourselves, to douse the doubt? Courage!

Courage is a funny thing—it's like quality—we may not know how to define it but we definitely know it when we see it. Courage is akin to grasping a cloud—it's elusive, mysterious, and it effortlessly changes form. When we're in the midst of a very challenging situation, we're too preoccupied (and often too overwhelmed) with the circumstances to stop and evaluate our actions as courageous or otherwise; which makes this a time-sensitive quality, as well. We can usually recognize our courageous acts only in hindsight, when we rewind the tape of our lives and evaluate the data.

I suspect that if we knew, in advance, just what it would take to move that mountain, then none of us would do a single, solitary thing—that we would, quite literally, frighten ourselves into inertia. How many times have we reflected to ourselves, "It's a good thing I didn't know how hard it was going to be or I wouldn't have done it."

Rarely are we actually able to anticipate our own courage, nor do we consciously do something with courage as our end objective. The courage part was mostly accidental, which does not imply that we can't learn to engage our courage at will—because we can. It's simply that the courage was the sizzle, not the steak.

> Courage is that bridge between believing and knowing.

Contemporary courage has nothing to do with wrestling criminals to the ground or saving children from burning buildings; those are, by and large, instinctual fight or flight responses. The courage that's most tantalizing to discuss and most tempting to imitate is found in ordinary women who live extraordinary lives.

What *is* an extraordinary life? One that you're 100 percent at choice about! And "courage" is a choice! An extraordinary life looks exactly and precisely like you planned it. It feels like you want it to feel and it looks the way you want it to look. Every detail is configured to support you and your life purpose. An extraordinary life means that you are giving yourself, allowing yourself the permission, the trust, the love, and the courage to live invincibly.

Extraordinary women are those who recognize and own that they are at choice about their own happiness: These women are willing to risk whatever discomfort, pain, and safety net in order to vote for themselves and say yes to their lives. The most invincible women are the ones who pay small attention to what they "should" be doing and how it "will look" to others: They seek only to walk their own path, to fulfill their own purpose, and to leave their impact wherever they go.

> We learn that courage is being who we are. It is being authentic.

There is nothing authentic about being invisible, or not trusting yourself with your own life when you know darn well that your inner wisdom and your intuition are more reliable than the car you're driving. There is nothing authentic about pretending that you're not infinitely powerful so that those around you won't feel uncomfortable. Go ahead; let them be uncomfortable. Don't take that gift from them; it may be just what they need to encourage them to emulate you and find their own path, their own purpose, their own power, just as you once did.

As we evolve from invisible to invincible and expand into all that we are capable of being, we become exponentially more invested in the choices we make: We more fully comprehend the impact those choices have had within us and around us. So make great ones!

Initiate Impact!

1. How does the way you trust yourself impact your ability to perform at your job?
2. Who do you know whose self-trust you would like to model?
   - Why them?
   - What would you do differently in your life right now?
3. If you took all your courage and applied it to your personal life, what would be different?
   - How would you change it?
4. What is the most courageous thing you have ever done?
   - Why did you do what you did?
   - What did you learn about yourself from doing it?
   - How can you apply that learning to other situations?

Essay 29

"Rejection Is God's Way of Saving You the Trouble"

Valuing Your Failures

Butch was one of the best tour guides I've ever had, except he wasn't actually a tour guide. He was my driver and we were on our way from the airport to the River Walk in San Antonio. On a gorgeous fall day in 2007, Butch made sure I was fully aware of every last exciting thing "The Alamo City" had to offer. He wasn't aware that I would only be in his friendly city less than 24 hours while I was delivering a keynote.

When we had almost reached our destination, Butch glanced back at me and excitedly urged me to look out the rear window at the Alamodome.

Butch: Hurry, before we pass it completely. It's the tan building.
Me: The Alamodome? I don't see it. Which one is it?
Butch: Right behind you.
Me: Describe it to me.
Butch: It's the one that looks like an upside down armadillo.
Me: Butch, Butch, Butch. I'm from New York City. I don't even know what a right side up armadillo looks like.

Perspective

Former CEO of Hewlett-Packard Carly Fiorina remarked on being publicly fired in February 2005: "I didn't fail. I was fired."

Perspective

Whenever I have the good fortune to speak to a room filled with women, we inevitably end up in a conversation about relationships—the romantic kind. Regardless of the number of women in attendance—10, 100, or 1,000—at least half of them will volunteer that they are divorced. When I then ask how many of them knew before their nuptials that they shouldn't marry the person they subsequently divorced, about 90 percent of the initial half will keep their hands in the air! What do they have to say about that? After a wave of nervous giggling, they'll share:

- "I knew in my heart it wasn't right; but he looked so good on paper."
- "I knew he had a problem with drinking, gambling, womanizing, debt, and/or _____; but he didn't stay out all night, beat me, treat me disrespectfully, and/or _____—so I rationalized that it would be okay."
- "My mother told me I had unrealistic expectations and I was being too picky."

Here's the high voltage questions: Should these women focus on the fact that their marriage failed, and that they failed? Or should they, instead, be congratulating themselves on having known better than to marry in the first place? They knew, in their hearts, that they weren't making a powerful decision for themselves and they married anyway, in essence, ignoring their inner wisdom. So did they *really* fail, or is this 'failed marrriage' further evidence for them to own what they know in the future and unreservedly trust themselves? It's a matter of **perspective**, isn't it?

Perspective

■ ■ ■

It's *our* viewpoint, *our* outlook, *our* position, *our* attitude, or *our* interpretation. *"We see life as we are."*

The singular distinction between success and failure lies between our ears. We see life through our unique lens; you will never meet another person who will see your life precisely as you do.

Failure is generally seen as a lack of success. It's an omission or neglect in fulfilling some promise. I'll give you that. Now tell me, what is a success? It's what we think it is, correct? At a time when we have been conditioned to look outside ourselves for feedback and input, this presents a challenge—because the only one who can define failure or success for you is you! But we typically catalog failures as those events having outcomes other than the ones we'd wanted.

Note: Absence of success isn't evidence of failure. There is no failure; there is only feedback.

Failure, like courage, should be determined over a protracted period of time. What looks like a failure today could actually be a godsend tomorrow. Think about a time when you didn't get the job you wanted, and six months later a better one came along. How about that relationship that you thought you'd perish without? And along came Mr. or Mrs. Right some time later; and you were oh so glad that you'd been "rejected" a few months before. An acquaintance of mine slipped into a noticeable funk when he was outbid on his dream house. Woe was he. Not a year later, the house literally blew to smithereens because of an undetected gas leak. Thankfully, no one was home.

I have witnessed this phenomenon many, many times in my life and in the lives of my friends and clients. I have accrued enough confirmation to lead me to conclude that if an event doesn't transpire as I'd hoped at some point, down the road I will be grateful that it didn't. Garth Brooks says "Thank God for Unanswered Prayers." Nancy Solomon says, "***Rejection is God's way of saving you the trouble.***"

There are few tools as valuable as the ability to reframe the circumstances of our lives; to consciously and courageously choose an empowering and impactful perspective over its disempowering and victimizing counterpart.

This is not to say that in the midst of the experience, we should go straight to the 10,000-foot view, nor does it assume that we even can. We're human. We may first need to have our temper tantrum, hissy fit, crying session, pity party—whatever it is that will help us to fully experience the event at every emotional level. If we don't process those feelings at the time we feel them, you can be assured that they will eventually be processed. But, like taxes, you may pay interest and penalties. Once we've had our emotional catharsis, we can then choose to reframe the event. You will be amazed at how invincible you will feel when you realize that this event, like most others, turned out to be a gift.

We are meaning-making machines; every single bit of information that we process is assigned a subjective value that is consistent with our belief system. Some of these values are obvious to us, while others pass us by with scant attention paid to them. The occurrences in our lives, our unintended outcomes included, can be placed into three distinct buckets:

+ The event that took place.
+ The meaning or interpretation we assign to the event (such as the 'failed' marriage perspective discussed earlier in this essay).
+ Who we became as a result of the event (how this event impacted us)

> "Who we become *as a result of the experience—not the experience itself—* is most valuable."
> —Nancy D. Solomon

The value of failure lies in this last and most crucial point. If you reflect back on your own history, you're likely to find that those opportunities in which you might not have succeeded but in which you also changed in some vital and positive way are no longer mentally or emotionally classified as failures. These are now "learning opportunities," "times of growth," and "transition periods." Ask yourself:

+ How did this experience change you?
+ How did it alter your life and your future?

- What tools did you gather in the process; and how do you use them now?
- Who would you have been without this experience? How do you know that?
- How did the overall experience impact you?

When we witness our life as a series of experiences that influence, shape, and press us to become more of who we were meant to be—then we can shift our thinking from "what's wrong with us" to *"what's right with us."* We can begin to perceive all the events that didn't turn out as we'd planned, and that fell short of our expectations, as the times when we received what we needed, though not necessarily what we wanted. These events now become *"causes for celebration instead of opportunities for apology."*

> *"Our journey is about becoming who we were meant to be. The experiences are the vehicles that get us there."*
> —Nancy D. Solomon

Life is *not* about what we do; life is about who we become. This necessarily implies that our focus—the lens with which we view ourselves if we want to maximize our impact—needs to be on who we are evolving into as people, instead of solely on what we do in the material world. The invitation this presents is for us to discover where we're going *and* whom we need to become in order to get there. Then, and only then, should we focus on what we need to do to achieve that goal.

Initiate Impact!

Use Figure 29.1 as a guide. Make a list of several of the so-called failures or disappointments in various areas of your life. Identify the patterns and write about what you've come to realize.

The Event "The Failure"	Your Reaction When It Happened	How You Feel About It Now	What You Learned
Laid off from job after fifteen years with the company.	**Fear:** How will I pay the mortgage? **Hurt:** I gave them everything I had! **Mad:** They should have laid off Jim!	**Relief:** I never liked that industry anyway. I'm so much happier now, in my new field.	**To trust myself:** I knew I should have left that job twelve years ago.

FIGURE 29.1   The Event vs. What You Learned Chart

Essay 30

"What if There's Nothing Wrong with You?"

Spiritual Permission

For much of my life I didn't believe in God, for what I thought was a perfectly justifiable reason: I was eight years old when my older brother died. He was about to turn ten. He was my hero, my protector, my best friend; when he died, I decided that I wasn't going to befriend any God who would take my Bruce from me. I later found out that God didn't really care whether I embraced Him or not; either way, He was here to stay.

I would never commit to print the things I did with the rage I carried about the loss of my brother. Let's just say that I got ample practice being my lowest life form. That bitter rage was not only self-destructive, it alienated me from the only source of comfort I can ever truly count on: my inner wisdom, spirit, higher self. The very thing I needed most in my life is what I pushed farthest away; which ultimately served only to proliferate the rage.

> *"We do what we do until it gets too painful or we get bored; and then we do something different."*
> —Nancy D. Solomon

For me, it was the former, and the "something different" was an excruciating and prolonged journey inward, precipitated by an eating disorder. Here's some of what I learned and what that has to do with God and permission.

It has been my experience that when we go to our place of worship—or to whatever that place is within ourselves where we communicate with God—we ask Him, or whatever we believe in, to grant us our prayers, dreams, hopes, and aspirations. We ask for these things as though they can actually be *given* to us; as though the power to create them lies solely "out there" instead of "in here." Not!

Growth takes guts. No small dose of self-awareness will help us realize that everything we've always wanted is already within us. Instead of praying for things, we might more effectively pray for the universe's *energetic support* in making those things manifest. Think: *The Wizard of Oz* and Dorothy clicking her heels together.

The spiritual aspect of permission is our ability to not only see ourselves as God does, but to create our lives in that image, to actually "hold" ourselves as source. Spiritual permission means that we *allow* the divine within us to flourish. It means we set aside our ego (aka—edging God out) to create an opening in our minds for our splendor, and in our lives for mystical inspiration. Spiritual permission allows us to live in a state of perpetual abundance and prosperity.

> Spiritual permission presumes that every last thing we will ever need is already in our possession; that it is already at our disposal, and all that is required for us to access it is for us to *get out of the way*.

When we grant ourselves spiritual permission, we're aligning all the components of our lives with our God-Self and our life purpose. The emotional commitment we make declares that we are deliberate in our intention that our mental and physical lives be congruent with our spirituality.

Our current global state of affairs, although not great from a financial perspective, has opened up the heart of the world. It has incited us to microscopically inspect and assess our lives, our priorities, our values; and most obviously, our impact (whose significance for women has exponentially grown in the past few years). The world is becoming increasingly polarized between the head and the heart; between what we think and how we feel; between our spirituality/emotions and the mental/physical.

It is not in the province of this book to fully address this topic; briefly and simply, what this looks like in your world is this: One cohort lives from the inside out, and the other lives from the outside in. The former are those who I mentioned a bit earlier—those determined to create their lives from their inner wisdom and in alignment with their life purpose. This does not imply that these folks don't have great affection for the lovely things that money can buy; that simply isn't true. It merely indicates that their material world does not birth their life; instead, their life births their material world.

The latter, those living from the outside in, are more focused on what their world looks like than what it feels like. Think of the worst stereotype of Wall Street, and then back it up a bit. These people are, to a large degree, removed from their spirituality. *It's not that they aren't spiritual; spirituality is just not the compass for their lives.* This group's life purpose may or may not be important to them (or even in their consciousness), but regardless, it doesn't determine their commitment to their lives.

When we are living in spiritual permission, we allow ourselves to:

- Fulfill our genetic potential
- Feel and express every emotion in our heart
- Realize our physical potential
- Actualize our dreams
- Become an instrument of our purpose
- Actualize the God within us
- Be used for a greater purpose
- Stretch to the outer limits of who we are
- Have impact

Allowing; enabling; consenting in contrast to making, forcing, or doing. Stepping aside and just assuming the magic will happen. Not an easy task in a culture that rewards us action junkies for getting it done and making it happen; and is quick to mistake stillness or patience for laziness or ineptitude.

Allowing means that we can access the fullness of the person we were born to be, living into what we've been given. It means stepping into the privilege of ourselves and owning that the kingdom of wealth within us was meant to be tapped into, destined to be explored.

> *"Spiritual Permission: Where "I think I can"*
> *transforms into "I knew I could"!"*
> —Nancy D. Solomon

Sometimes we don't want to find the boundaries of our own greatness, because we're afraid of discovering that we might be as expansive as we thought we were. So we don't even attempt to do things because we don't want to be disappointed? What kind of attitude is that! If you revisit The Introduction, the discussion of regret, you'll recall that we learned that most people don't regret the things they've attempted. Rather, it's what they didn't attempt that disrupts their peace of mind. What I find to be true is that when we go for it and risk an unexpected outcome, we don't usually fail at all; we frequently discover that we're infinitely more powerful than we initially gave ourselves credit for.

If you retain little else, keep this close to you: We are not given a gift without the ability to use it. We are not given a dream without the possibility of fulfilling it. We are not given a life purpose without also being given everything we need to make it manifest.

> *"Permission is what bridges our gifts with*
> *our life purpose."*
> —Nancy D. Solomon

Spiritual Permission is when we are at our most powerful; when we let the world see what we're made of; when we display our limitlessness; when we stop pretending that we are a refrigerator bulb when we are actually a stadium light. I'd like to show you what that looks like—meet Marilyn.

More than anything else, Marilyn wanted to be a weekly contributor to her local business newspaper. She approached the publisher, a man she'd met several times while networking, and he told her that he didn't have a market for what she offered: "Women in business is not a top priority of ours," he said. At first, Marilyn was stunned with disbelief. Women in business weren't a top priority? Under what rock had this man been sleeping? Then she sulked: She knew her skills far exceeded those of the three people who already wrote for the paper and her expertise, women, couldn't be more timely. Two weeks after she was rejected Marilyn gave herself a reality check and acknowledged that the only reason she wanted to write for the local paper was that she was too scared to do what she *really* wanted to do—write for a national publication. Retrieving her self-confidence, Marilyn approached three national newspapers—two offered her a column. Why were her services refused on a local level? It was her spirit telling her she was destined for greater things.

> *"Perhaps you're uncomfortable not because your vision is too big, but because you're standing in a place too small."*
> —Nancy D. Solomon

I'm sure you've noticed that spiritual permission just assumes that your impact is already a done deal; that there is something to get out of the way of; that when you pull the plug, something of great value will automatically flow. We'd be immeasurably happier and more culturally successful if we'd just assume that we're amazing creatures—honestly. The fact is that, as human beings, we make up all this stuff anyway; we subjectively assign meaning to every iota of information that we process: 20 million bits of information a second. So why not interpret things to highlight our personal power, instead of making up stuff that makes us feel small, insignificant, and puny? And how about we start doing that today?

The universe provides us with a physical picture of our mental and emotional expectations. This means that whatever we look for, we are guaranteed to see. If we focus our attention on the divinity within us, on the seed of greatness we carry, on the spark of genius in our minds, then our physical world will aptly reflect that. Likewise, if we focus on the things that disturb us, upset us, make us feel worthless and undeserving, then that will, in short order, become our experience.

Years ago, I was preparing for a training session in the ballroom of a major hotel. I had five or six people assisting me and, as the evening wore on, I began to notice that their enthusiasm for setting up the room was waning with the hour. I called the group together and, though tempted, decided to say nothing about the sloppiness of their preparation. I addressed these colleagues, who I knew were all Christians, by saying, "It is growing late and you are tired. Here's what I'd like you to do: Please prepare this room with 100 chairs assuming that, tomorrow, Christ will be sitting in every single one of them."

I returned one hour later to an immaculate space. Everything was in its perfect place, the room was spotless, and the energy was humming. What happened? I invited these fabulous folks to a place within them that already existed. Their only job was to match their experience of the room with their internal experience of Christ. That is spiritual permission; allowing our outside worldly experience to perfectly match the Greater Light within us.

The spiritual aspect of permission obliges us to stand in our own light, unapologetically using every gift, every talent, every watt of brilliance within us so we can bring the contribution that we are to the world. It means celebrating our own quirkiness, eccentricity, and unique personal brand. It is the quintessential observance of the wonder of us, of our life, and of what we've chosen to do with it. Permission lives in a state of grace and abundance. Giving ourselves permission says that we know our value and, in that, it is a state of entitlement—yet there is no ego in it

> It urges us to assess ourselves from the bias of what's right with us, and to give scant attention to those things we've decided (or have been told) are wrong with us, and need to be "fixed."

It insists that we view our lives through the lens of love, compassion, forgiveness, and benevolence.

We give ourselves spiritual permission when:

- We go for that job just beyond our reach.
- Our teenage daughter chews us up and spits us out—and we still take her to the mall.
- We forgive a colleague for some indiscretion, real or perceived.
- We give of ourselves when we're sure there's nothing left to give.
- We decline a promotion because our Inner Light gives it a thumbs down.
- We trust ourselves when the evidence would advise us against it.
- We return the extra 17 cents the cashier gave us.
- Our spouse acts sophomoric and we forgive what happened the minute we get an apology.
- We quiet ourselves in prayer and follow the guidance we receive regardless of how crazy it seems.
- The person in front of us is most unlovable—and we love him or her anyway.

■ ■ ■

Permission isn't an activity, an occasion, or an event; it is a mindset, a lifestyle, and an attitude that we deliberately choose. Our actions are restricted only by what we think. Our minds are burdened only by what we're unwilling to feel.

> Giving ourselves permission to get done what we came here to do is the ultimate expression of gratitude.

It says, "Thank you for allowing the flow of universal energy through me. I fully grasp how fortunate I am, how absolutely blessed I've been, to have been given this (fill in the blank) _____ _____ opportunity, gift, skill. I will stand in that gratitude by sharing myself with the world; not in a grandiose or inflated way, but with humility and awe. I will demonstrate my appreciation by being who I was meant to be by taking full advantage of this gift; and I will always cherish it."

There is a delicate balance between owning our worth and flaunting that ownership. Permission is the definitive line upon either side that these two rest. We're an instrument of the universe by living our appreciation, by expressing our gratitude; not by talking or bragging about it, complaining of its burden, or denying others their instrumentality. When we live in a state of permission, we take nothing for granted; we live in the spirit of generosity, and we invite those around us to do the same.

Spiritual permission insists that we focus solely on who we are; it is the number one singular distinction between those women who are invisible and those who are invincible.

Initiate Impact!

1. In what ways do you stand in the way of your life purpose?
2. Where do you need to give yourself permission to fulfill your mission?
3. What evidence of spiritual permission do you have in your life?
4. What negative assumptions do you need to drop in order to give yourself spiritual permission to be who you were meant to be?
5. If you were to fully relax into and live out of spiritual permission, what would your life feel like and look like?

Essay 31

"You Get in Life What You Have the Courage to Ask For"[*]

Asking for What You Want

Several years ago I received a call from an organization in search of a keynoter for their yearly event. We spent 30 minutes or so discussing the organization's needs for the evening, and filling in all the customary blanks in a reciprocal interview. Once we established that there was a great fit between us, the woman asked about my fee. I quoted my standard for a keynote, at which point she went silent.

Mary: Nancy, I know you're worth it because I've heard you speak, but I just don't have that size investment in my budget. Would you consider doing it for half price? It would be great exposure for you!

Me: I'd love to work with you and your organization and it's kind of you to make that offer, but I can't accept it.

Mary: That's too bad. I was really counting on having you speak.

Me: I'll tell you what, Mary, I'll do it for free.

Mary: For free? You'll do it for free? Why would you do that?

Me: Let me tell you where I'm coming from. If I cut my fee by 50 percent, I will still put in the same hours of preparation, and I will still be giving you the identical keynote as if you were

[*]Nancy D. Solomon

198

paying the full price. Here's my predicament: At the end of my keynote, it will have been so fantastic that you may be embarrassed that you didn't pay my full fee. What's more, I'm likely to feel resentful for having discounted my fee and, therefore, having discounted my services and myself. I set aside a certain number of hours each month for pro bono work. Let's just call this that, and then both of us will feel good about our decision to work together.

Mary: Yes, I see what you're saying. Let me think about this and I'll call you back tomorrow, okay?

Me: I'll look forward to it.

The following day Mary called and offered me my full fee. We discussed how she made this happen, and her feelings about it. I accepted. Suffice it to say that at the end of the keynote Mary ran up and hugged me. She whispered in my ear, "I didn't pay you enough for that very important lesson. Thank you!"

Now before you decide that I'm full of myself, let me say that I didn't do this so that Mary would return to her board begging for more budget. That's called manipulation and we don't even want to go there. I did it because I really wanted to speak to her organization *and* because of exactly what I told her *and* I would have been a hypocrite to stand before 500 women and talk to them about personal power and leadership after agreeing to take a 50 percent cut in my fee. Was I happy to get paid what I'm worth? Of course. Would I have done it for free? With pleasure.

Inadvertently, when we offer a **dis**-kount (discount) we're at risk of dis-**kounting** (discounting) ourselves. No one should believe in you more than you do. The clearest, most efficient way to communicate our self-worth is by asking for what we want.

Many women habitually order short: We take what we're given, instead of asking for what we want.

This sends a disempowering message to the world and to ourselves. Then, we either realize we've done this and get angry with ourselves, or we fail to recognize what we've done and resent the person who "did it" to us. Repeat after me, "There are no victims."

Note: Just because you ask for something doesn't mean you're guaranteed to get it. However, *"the answer to every question you don't ask is 'No.'"*

Elaine is a superstar employee in the company she has worked at for only 18 months. She works long hours, gives it her all, frequently volunteers first for extra projects, and overall is one of those high potential employees everyone prays for. Did I mention that her can-do attitude has been contagious in her division?

Elaine came to coaching to strategically plan her career. Traditional career planning is *not* my expertise: Elaine felt that she'd not progressed in her career as well as she could have because of some childhood experiences which had left her low on confidence and high on trauma. She wanted a reality check.

I am a big picture thinker used to making long range plans, so Elaine and I mapped out where she wanted to be in five years, why she wanted to be there, precisely what she would need to accomplish during that time, and the skill sets she'd need to acquire. We then put together a comprehensive plan including mentors, two to four levels up, for each of the skill sets she'd need. A few months into the process, Elaine concluded that, in an ideal world, she would report three levels over her manager to the executive vice president of the organization. That's where self-confidence needed to be factored in.

"You get in life what you have the courage to ask for."

Such a move was beyond a stretch of her imagination. Standard practice was a one-level-up move every 18 months and no one had ever, in the company's history, reported up from her level to EVP. Elaine made a case, rehearsed until she was flawless, and approached the EVP. He agreed with her! Not only that, but he volunteered to make things right with her manager, so he would not be offended. She's currently on track, two years ahead of her five-year plan.

> How did she do that? Instead of asking herself "why" the company would say yes, she asked herself, "why wouldn't they?"

Have you ever wanted something but, for some reason, you were reluctant to ask for it and then someone you knew asked and he or she got it? If we don't ask for what we want, then one of two things will happen: We will either transform into victims because no one can read our minds to discover what we really want (how *could* they not know!); or, we can pretend that *had* we asked we might have gotten what it was we wanted. Here's the accountability piece: When we actually do ask for what we want, then we have a chance for someone to say no, at which point we can either choose to feel rejected or choose to congratulate ourselves for the courage it took to ask in the first place.

This could be something small like asking for that last piece of pie or returning your meal in a restaurant because it didn't meet your expectations. It could also be something large like a raise (when there are no discretionary dollars in the budget), an increase over last year's order from your customer (even though business is soft), or like Elaine a daring career move that could have, possibly, offended a number of very influential people.

> Why do we order short? Why don't we ask for what we want? Fear.

Fear that we'll be rejected, we'll look stupid, we'll be inappropriate, no one will like us, or there's a perfectly good reason but no one sent you the memo so you didn't know. *And what if you get what you ask for and you don't know what to do with it?* Then, of course, there's always the I-don't-deserve demon and the I'm-not-worthy witch, both of whom collude with your ego to ensure that you'll stay an invisible victim.

Add to that mix the fact that women tend not to promote their own interests (see Essay #14), instead focusing on the needs of others, often to their detriment. Let's not forget those of us who have been penalized as pushy when we do ask for what we want. Remember? We're too ambitious! That explains it!

Linda Babcock and Sara Laschever, in their book, *Women Don't Ask*, cite a now well-known study of graduate MBAs from Carnegie Mellon. The starting salaries of the graduating males were 7.6 percent higher, or almost $4,000 more than the graduating females from the same program. Why would that be? It's easy to assume that it's gender inequity, isn't it? That was my first thought. But, no, it's because *the women didn't ask for more*; the average woman accepted the employer's initial salary offer and only 7 percent of the women actually negotiated their salary. The men, on the other hand, negotiated for a figure closer to their ideal; a whopping 57 percent negotiated.

Has there been a time when you didn't ask for a raise because you knew there wasn't any money in the budget? Or because someone needed it more than you did? Or because you were feeling shy, and not really sure you deserved it? What should you do? Get yourself some great books or take a class on the art and science of negotiation. Put this on the top of your to-do list because we are all negotiating all the time. Jeanette Nyden, a negotiation expert and professional mediator, recently published *Negotiation Rules! A Practical Approach to Big Deal Negotiations* (Sales Gravy Press, 2009). You'll want to read it!

Contemplate this: What if you ask for what you want, you get it, and you're hugely successful? What about that option? What if the world is just sitting back waiting for you to request away?

What if you are lucky enough, courageous enough, spunky enough, to meet someone like my new friend, Jim Everett? Let me tell you about him and how we met.

A few months before this book was to be published, I decided to name *Impact's* web site and blog *From Invisible to Invincible.com*. No brainer, right? Sure enough, it belonged to someone else, and that someone else was Jim Everett. My intuition clearly told me that this was to be my URL, so I looked him up and I called him. A voice mail or two later, I told Jim why I was calling and that I would love to become the proud owner of *his* URL.

I'm laughing as I'm relating this story because Jim is a soft-spoken Midwesterner, nice as the day is long, and I am a New Yorker with *big* energy. I was so excited that he took my call that the entire time we were talking I was taking deep meditative breaths so I wouldn't overwhelm him. Jim's business is called From Invisible to In Demand Marketing.com, which explains his ownership of *my* URL. At first, he wasn't terribly thrilled with what I was proposing. At one point I believe he actually said no. I remember having read something Jeanette Nyden once said about shutting up once you put your offer on the table, so I didn't back down (yes, I was nervous). We ended our conversation after I pressed him a bit to think about it overnight, and with plans for me to call him the following day. I then wrote Jim an e-mail expressing my gratitude for his consideration of my request. Here is the e-mail I received from Jim the very next morning:

Hi Nancy,

I spent some time alone yesterday to make sure to get in touch with the best decision regarding this URL. I have decided that it's not for sale, and I'm not going to trade it. However, I will give it to you with no strings attached. After considering your offer, I realized that I don't want to be mentioned in your book as part of a trade. The only condition under which I would ever want to be mentioned is because I did something of value AND because it made a better book. This is purely at your discretion and I have no interest in influencing you. . . .

The reason I'm doing this is because I believe you have something great here and the consistent message will help you to impact the lives of many people. I am happy to make this small contribution of transferring this URL to you.

"You get in life what you have the courage to ask for."

Now that's a story worth repeating!

Jim and I are now fast becoming friends, collaborating on some programs, and teaching each other the things each of us knows best. What did I learn?

- If we want something, anything, we have to ask for it. It's a choice.
- This world is going to be as kind, compassionate, and encouraging as we will allow it to be, and not one iota more.
- Collaboration can happen wherever we are; we just have to open the door.
- When our intentions are in integrity with our life purpose, the universe conspires in some interesting ways to support us.

Now I have the opportunity to pay Jim's kindness forward the next time someone asks me to do something that I might, initially, be disinclined to do. So, at the end of the day, Jim gave me much, much more than a URL, didn't he? Much more, in fact, than *I'd* even had the courage to ask for.

Initiate Impact!

1. What is one opportunity in your life, right now, that you're eager to take advantage of?
2. What is standing in your way of going for it?
3. What outrageous request do you need to make in order for that to happen?
4. Who can support you in your efforts?
5. Name one reason that you wouldn't ask for what you want.
6. Now name one regret you'll have if you don't.

Part Five

Impact at Work

Essay 32

From the Ironing Board to the Board Room

Business Is Personal

Editor: Is *Impact!* a business book or a self-help book?

Me: Yes!

Editor: It can't be both. It's either a business book or a self-help book. What shelf in the bookstores do you want to see it on?

Me: Both. As a woman in business, I don't want to have to choose between the two. When I help myself, I help my business, don't I? After all, it is my 'Self' who's conducting the business, isn't that so? *Impact!* needs to be in both places, just like I am. In fact, it *must* be in both places because it's timely, relevant, and current. Just like we women are!

Editor: Sigh.

■ ■ ■

Business life. Personal life.

Don't you find it intriguing that we perversely cling to the idea that they are mutually exclusive? In this day and age, I wonder why we continue to think that these two vital components of our lives should be kept separate. I'm equally perplexed that there are some people who believe that there are benefits to be reaped by pretending that business and personal matters actually *can* be segregated; that it's even possible should we decide it's advantageous. Which it most certainly is not.

> Divorcing our business from our personal life is as archaic and ludicrous as designating specific colors or jobs as either male or female.

In every other area of our lives, we're demanding that boundaries become more fluid and malleable than ever before. Consider this: Pink used to be a woman's color until it became the new black for men's shirting. Gardening used to be women's play until it was monetized, and then it became men's work too. Attorneys were, historically, men and now women earn half the seats in law school. You get the point.

I grew up, professionally, at a time when people were defined, in absolute terms, by the nature of their work or their business. It was implicitly understood that our work and our identity were synonymous. Those 50, 60, 70 hours a week were *it*—it's what gave us our self-esteem, our self-worth, our value. Everything else in our lives, by default, was dismissed as frivolous.

It's one life we have, isn't it? To be sure, there will be times when one aspect obscures the other, or when the challenges in one part of our life bleed onto its neighbor. But life, in general, is just life.

The separation was initially born in an era when business was for boys and emotions were for girls. Which, in sexist lingo, means that business was the important stuff and the personal was merely fluff. Today we call that bad business. Today we're all a-twitter with this new concept called relationship marketing—marketing that is based on and has evolved out of our need to emotionally connect to one another (and our selves, I might add).

Let's back up a moment, shall we?

Take a moment and define business. _____
_____
_____
_____

Take another moment and define personal. _____
_____
_____
_____

What did you learn?
What beliefs do you have about both of these?

Pardon me if I seem a bit simple—I am not—but I am on a mission to persuade you, encourage you, and coerce you into rethinking the way you relate to both aspects of your life, and how both aspects correlate with one another.

At its most fundamental:

- Business is conducted by people.
- Business provides people with a service or product.
- Business provides people with jobs for which they earn compensation.
- People impact their own businesses and the businesses of others.
- People are *also* impacted by their own businesses, and the businesses of others.

Think reciprocity!

If our selves, as human beings, are the ones who are inextricably enmeshed in business, then logic follows that anything that helps us, supports us, educates us, validates us, assists us, in any way, impacts how we do business, why we do business, and the bottom line of that business, as well.

Self-help is business help because *who we are impacts everything we do.*" If it impacts us, it impacts our business.

There can be no distinction, despite what we've been told, how we've been trained, or why we deceived ourselves into thinking otherwise. To attempt, in any manner, to separate the personal from the business is arrogant at best and ignorant at worst.

My professional experience, as one of the people to whom businesses turn when the "soft issues" become agonizingly hard, has repeatedly reinforced my assertion that business is personal. Very personal.

The Great Divide, as I call it, is that invisible space where emotional currency is replaced by intellectual capital. It's the place where we ostensibly park our feelings at the door and pick up our professional personae at the same place. In truth, it is an abyss into which our most treasured values can potentially fall.

Thom works in a public accounting firm and has been a top-performing partner for the past 17 years. His company, like the competition, has been dramatically affected by recent economic events. Thom was recently called into his boss's office and, due to falling profits and much needed cutbacks, was told that he was being laid off. His boss, a gentleman he'd worked with for over five years, said "Thom, please don't take this personally, but the new budget demands that we trim our overhead, so we're letting you go."

Does Thom now go to his bank and say to them, "Please don't take this personally, but I can't pay my mortgage and I just know you'll understand?" Of course not! Was Thom's career impacted by this corporate decision? Yes! Therefore, did it impact his personal life? You bet!

Most of us wouldn't go through the futile exercise of trying to pinpoint the precise place where the personal ends and the business begins. What is evident is that the more we've answered life's call, the more we're living our life purpose and following our passion, the harder it is to distinguish what is personal from what is not. We just *are*. No clear delineation is required. No clear distinction really exists.

Where does feeling end and thinking begin? It doesn't: Business begins and ends with us: every holistic cell of us. There is a plethora of research that has unequivocally concluded that feelings override rational decision-making. Hands down. It's not even a conversation anymore according to most studies.

I'm prompted to inquire as to what it is about the prospect of our feelings and our fragile psyches that's so uncomfortable for us that we are willing to perpetuate the myth that good business excludes the mother of all motivators—emotions.

What I've observed, an unpleasant number of times, is that people use the "it's just business" rationale as a catchall excuse when they don't want to take responsibility for dealing with feelings they're uncomfortable with. So "Don't take this personally" becomes the repository for the emotions the owner has yet to metabolize. While you may enthusiastically be reading a business self-help book, there are many people who would rather climb a 10,000-foot mountain barefoot than deal with the complexity of their feelings. I work with these folks every day. Unfortunately, they are not an anomaly.

■ ■ ■

The current economic debacle that has overtaken us is doing a fine job of shaking things up; some of which needed shaking and others, not so much. We've produced the perfect storm in which to reexamine our lives, elucidate our values and narrow the gap between our espoused beliefs and our embodied ones. Lest we fall into victimization and blame, every one of us needs to own our part in this financial fiasco. It's not just those in the C-Suite who pulled the wizard's curtain shut. We watched them do it.

Why are we here? What caused us to spend beyond our means, accept large amounts of bonus money while not achieving our organizational goals, and extend credit to people who hadn't yet earned it?

Ego.

And ego is personal. Ego may impinge itself on business, but it grew out of our psychological need, not our intellectual one: Our need to have a bigger title than the person in the next cubicle, to make more money than our colleague, to have more direct-reports than the other award-winning high potential newbie. This ego affliction is not confined to executives; it's endemic to every corporate culture. Ego speaks of our self-importance, self-aggrandizement, self-centeredness, self-image, self-absorption, and self-worth.

Self.

Personal. Emotional. Nary a mention of business.

> The global economy has caused businesses to become more holistic than ever. The recent ethics and moral scandals have stimulated us to reexamine and to establish more congruence throughout our lives.

Add to that mix Gen X and Gen Y, with their allegiance to their lifestyle, and I can't imagine us reverting to the segregation of our day job from the rest of our lives. We're in global economic purgatory because of some insatiable need to feed our egos, not because we're intellectual imbeciles. So let us stop fantasizing. Our personal lives and our professional lives go together like peanut butter and jelly.

Initiate Impact!

1. How does who you are, at your core, impact your career?
2. Which of your core personality traits enhance your job and improve your performance?
3. Which traits hinder your career and negatively impact your performance?

4. What is one event in your personal life that profoundly impacted your career?
   + What happened and what was the consequence?
5. What one event in your career profoundly impacted your personal life?
   + What happened and what was the consequence?

Essay 33

The Emotional Economy

Emotions Drive Decision-Making

Relationships can make people edgy and uncomfortable. Especially in business. They necessarily imply emotion, and emotion is a messy subject. It suggests chaos, upheaval, lack of control, and weakness—traits traditionally feared for their potentially negative impact on the bottom line. Numbers are nice and neat. They either add up or they don't. Not so with people. And people are my passion.

Not once has it failed to simultaneously cause me to grimace and giggle when I'm introduced to an organization or at a conference as the woman who handles the soft issues. Granted, gone are the jeers from the 1980s and 1990s, yet I must still endure the knowing nod in my direction that is the non-physical equivalent of a pat on my pretty little head. Their unspoken speech bubble would read, "Now run along, little lady, and go play with HR." Condescending. Self-righteous. Superior. The corresponding speech bubble over said pretty little head would read, "The soft issues are really the complex issues, which is why no one wants to deal with them!"

That said, emotions as *the* barometer of relationships in business has dramatically changed in the past 10 to 15 years. Science has partnered with the psychology of performance and has provided us with stacks of statistics from institutions as old as money and as reliable as taxes. They all say the same thing: Logic does not lead. Emotions do.

> We make emotional choices and then back them up with logic, reason, and data. Yes, even in business.

Had these researchers conferred with me I would have been the voice reminding them that *business is personal* (see Essay #32), which is why our emotions are far more reliable indicators than a lot of research is. But they didn't.

For the past 15-plus years, the field of cognitive neuroscience has greatly expanded our understanding of the impact that emotions have on human learning and communications. The Gallup Organization used these recent discoveries and integrated them with similar work in the fields of psychology, economics, and social sciences. Gallup conducted an in-depth study of human behavior from 1997 to 2001, interviewing almost 10 million customers on their opinions, attitudes, feelings, and behaviors.[1] Among the study's conclusions:

- Emotions drive our decision-making.
- Emotions take place outside our rational, willful awareness.
- Emotional engagement increases the speed of learning, increases memory retention, and evokes emotions in others.

The conclusion? We are emotionally based beings. What we feel is more important than what we think. Every decision we make is in pursuit of an emotional goal. Our emotions dictate our decisions, not the other way around. Our emotions translate into every choice we make in our lives. And while it really seems quite simple, this not-so-newfound philosophy has shaken the foundation of American business.

---

[1] Curt Hoffman and Gabriel Gonzalez-Molina. *Follow This Path: How the World's Greatest Organizations Drive Growth by Unleashing Human Potential.* (New York: Warner Books, Inc., 2002).

> The data we have is tumbling the antiquated patriarchy that was emotionally incompetent, un-savvy in relationship skills, and too darned frightened of anything related to feelings to pay any attention to the obvious—that people are human beings first and everything else second.

As we women continue to infiltrate the highest ranks of leadership in corporate America, emotion-based conversations are becoming less of an anomaly and more of a competitive advantage. Did I hear someone say, "It's about time"?

We have learned that consumers make purchases in pursuit of the emotional experience they seek. They return to the same businesses and become loyal to brands because of the way these businesses and brands make them feel. People buy products, mortgage homes, choose partners, develop hobbies, bank with certain institutions, and select their favorite grocery stores because these choices evoke desired feelings. Loyalties develop when people feel emotionally invested—engaged—in the outcome they attain. Turn the relationship dial up one more notch and you move from loyal to devoted; to that platinum customer who sings your praises from the rooftop, to whom you can do no wrong, and who is the bread-and-butter ambassador of referrals for a steady stream of new likeminded customers. Think: Costco, Apple's iTunes and iPhone, Target, Nordstrom. Ahh!

Although there has been a profusion of new information on consumer buying habits published in the past several years, one of the most conclusive studies was completed by the University of Florida in 2002.[2] This national study analyzed the responses of 23,168 people to 240 advertising messages in 13 categories as diverse as cars and appliances, groceries, and other small-ticket items. The results, which appeared in the August 2002 issue of *Journal of Advertising Research*, concluded that emotions were nearly twice as important as knowledge

---

[2]Jon D. Morris, Chongmoo Woo, James Geason, and Jooyoung Kim. "The Power of Affect: Predicting Intention," *Journal of Advertising Research* (2003), 1–14.

in consumer buying decisions—that individuals may be interested in the technical aspect of a purchased item, but this interest is driven by the desire to achieve a specific emotional response. This evidence refutes the historical data that strongly implied that consumers made their purchases based on information, data, and logical conclusions and that if emotions were involved at all, it was purely incidental.

Apparently these researchers hadn't shopped with a woman before! In 2008 we women were responsible for 88 percent of all consumer spending—$3.7 trillion. We also spent $44.5 billion on office supplies, $55 billion on electronic products (51 percent), and 83 cents of every household dollar. We have been very busy, haven't we?

There is a direct and suggestive correlation between the results of this study and the people who are your employees, colleagues, and coworkers. Your employees are consumers, too! Not just of your product or service, but of your brand in its entirety. To the greatest extent possible, you want everyone in your universe to drink the company Fruity-Fruit. Recently I spoke with the president of one of my client companies. I asked about a particular employee who had been struggling in his leadership position. The president responded by saying, "He's been promoted to customer." I'm not as quick as you are—it took me a moment to get that the man had been terminated, and that the company was now focused on converting him into a raving fan.

We may choose to indulge ourselves in "the facts" and try to convince ourselves that our decisions are logical and that we are, indeed, quite clever, but it is really our unconscious emotional tentacles that keep pulling us beyond our own reason, demanding such intangibles as happiness, satisfaction, and fulfillment.

> People choose a job in response to an emotional itch that needs scratching—and leave it for the very same reason.

Just as customers are courted with exceptional customer service, a superior product or service, and competitive pricing, employees are enticed with the prospect of feeling great about what they do, where they do it, and how much they are compensated for it. And what we know for sure is that the generations coming up through the workforce pipeline are insisting that their work environment provide them with emotional bennies.

There's no question about how the current global economic climate has impacted both employees and employers. But take heart—when we rebound, and we will, we'll be facing a whole new set of attraction and retention issues which will, once again, press us to clarify our value and our values. Those organizations that have shown respect and compassion for the people who, through no fault of their own were on the wrong end of the decision-making process when they were laid off, will have a wonderful situation to deal with: People will be standing in line to work for companies who put their people first, second, and third.

Then there are those businesses who treated their employees as commodities: They may find that they become overpopulated with low-hanging fruit—the disengaged and the people who are off-purpose. A short time ago, I got a frantic phone call from a client who had just had a one-on-one meeting with her manager. Long overdue for a promotion, she was told by her manager to sit tight and lower her expectations. He said, and I quote, "After all, it's an employer's market right now." Guess who will be looking for career advancement elsewhere as soon as that market opens up?

Now, more than ever, it's imperative that we return to the staples of business. What is at the very top of that list, what is most obvious, is this:

> Without people, who are fueled and propelled by their emotions, you don't even have a business. You have nothing, zero, zilch, nada, if you don't have a team of people invested in their relationship with you.

The very implication of managing emotions and relationships as tools for strategizing production and profit is a dramatic change from what we once thought to be true; a change that has only been fully embraced in the past several years. This is not going away, thank goodness. In the simplest terms, the information we now have indicates the desire for people to broaden their functional understanding of relationship, to expand their own relationship boundaries, and to become fully emotionally engaged at work, with their colleagues and with the company that employs them. This is true at any level of employment.

Our core has been captured: We are relational beings. We are concerned about our relationship with ourselves, our relationships with our family and friends, our relationships with our employees and employers, and our relationships with our customers.

We are responsible for our feelings. We value our intuition. We love our families and friends. We really want to be able to say that we love our jobs, although often we can't. We need to connect (see Essay #35) to feel life satisfaction. We want to bring all of ourselves to work. We're willing to give up a heck of a lot just to be happy.

> Fifty-two percent of us said we would trade a day's pay for a day off every week to have a more fulfilling, stress-free, and enjoyable life.

Perhaps it's not only emotionally engaged customers and employees that we seek. Perhaps we also seek to fully engage with our own lives before mortality makes that decision for us.[3]

Initiate Impact!

1. What have you noticed about the way your organization manages the relationships with its employees?
   - If you were making the decisions, what would you duplicate in your organization?
   - What would you do differently?

---

[3]Widmeyer Research & Polling. *Center for a New American Dream* (Washington, DC, August 2003).

2. If you look to the very top of your organization, how do those people impact your attitude about the organization and your job?
   - How do they treat the people in your organization?
3. What contribution do you make that positively impacts the company's ability to meet and exceed their goals.
   - How do you impact your co-workers' and customers' emotions about your company?
4. What might you do differently to insure that you positively impact your relationship with your colleagues and with your customers?

Essay 34

Getting Engaged
Engaged People Have More Impact

Once upon a time engagement was spoken about in relation to the size of the ring or the number of bridesmaids. It is now, of course, the organizational catchphrase that defines the depth and breadth of our involvement with our work and, subsequently, is a measure of our passion.

The concept of engagement is consuming our collective corporate bandwidth because of its implications for the bottom line. At it's most fundamental, engagement speaks to the relationship we have with our customers and to the extent to which they are inspired to do business with us as a result of that connection.

Our job, if we are to excel at it, is to build our customer's commitment and loyalty to our brand. Our job, when we are sincerely engaged in it, is to provide our employer with long-term value.

> Engagement is the metric for "how much skin we have in the game," how invested we are, and the depth and sustainability of that allegiance.

Engagement, in more personal terms, is the measure of the intimacy that we have with our world:

- How well do we know ourselves?
- Why might we be reluctant to be self-engaged?

- Do we know what our strengths are, what makes us happy, the value we place on our relationships, the things that de-motivate us?
- Do we know how we communicate our feelings, express our opinions, get heard when we're angry, and react when we're not?
- Do we focus on what's working or what's not, on what we have or what we don't?
- Can we tell when we're going through a transition, when we've given up or why we've let go?

> There is a direct and profound correlation between our level of engagement and our ability to positively impact the world.

Engagement is the diametrical opposite of invisibility, just as disengagement is the diametrical opposite of invincibility. In a sentence: If you want to make a personally meaningful difference, if you want to have sustainable impact, you simply *must* be self-engaged. *Note:* Self-engagement is a prerequisite for engagement at work. Since we are, practically speaking, the center of our own universe, our connection and, therefore, our engagement with others is an extension of, and a perfect mirror for, the one we have with ourselves.

The Gallup Organization's study referenced in Essay #33 concluded that 30 percent of all U.S. employees are engaged in their work, while 54 percent are not engaged, and 16 percent are actively disengaged.[1] The price tag for this lack of emotional commitment is about $250 billion a year.[2]

Disengaged people can be recognized by the manner in which they meander through their lives without purpose or passion. They show up,

---

[1] Coffman & Gonzalez-Molina, *Follow This Path: How the World's Greatest Organizations Drive Growth by Unleashing Human Potential.* (New York: Warner Books, Inc., 2002), p. 76.

[2] Jim Loehr and Tony Schwartz. *The Power of Full Engagement: Managing Energy, Not Time, Is the Key to Full Engagement and Optimal Performance* (New York: The Free Press, 2003).

get it done, and go home. "It" could be their job, their relationship, their parenting, their finances, their hobby, whatever. They lack urgency, commitment, devotion, and zest which is why, when you're with them, you may feel bored or distracted.

In Essay #18 I cited the astronomical cost of depression and presenteeism in the American workforce. I contend that much of our country's depression can be attributed to the disengagement of our population. I have yet to encounter a single person who was on purpose, fully engaged and irrevocably depressed. The question is—did depression lead to their disengagement or did disengagement manifest their depression? I would speculate that there is a blurred but reciprocal relationship between the two dynamics.

To be fair, every one of us periodically disengages throughout the course our lifetime. Surely we can't be "on" all the time, nor would we want to be—we would burn ourselves out before we hit 40. But there is a marked difference between pausing to recalibrate, rest, or retreat and taking a 30-year time-out because our lives, as we constructed them, were draining us dry.

The deliberate down times, the ones when we temporarily and consciously disengage, are vital to our creativity. Those of you who have ever driven a car with a manual transmission know that in order to change gears, you first have to shift to neutral. This applies to downshifting as well as upshifting. The same is true for people. Over the years I've seen countless people linger in neutral prior to making a personal evolutionary jump—I count myself as one of them. Sometimes we become fearful of the inactivity, of the inertia, and we bemoan our "stuck'" state. But we're not really stuck; we're just standing still while we gear up for the next engagement.

Picture if you will, the disengaged individual whose relationship with him or herself is depressed, dismal, distant, and dangerous. Dangerous? Yes! Imagine a driverless car veering down the highway at 90 miles an hour. It may go a short distance while only endangering itself, but at some point others will get sideswiped or killed by that out-of-control vehicle. So it is for so many of the disengaged. They are careening forward through their lives swept up by the momentum of those around them. At some point you will get caught up in the drama and dysfunction of their runaway life, and it will undoubtedly impact you. Not in a good way.

How do you recognize a disconnected, disengaged, and disheartened person in your life? The easiest answer is really a question: How do *you* feel when you're with this person? If you're inspired, excited, enthralled, and energized, it is likely that your friend is engaged. If, on the other hand, you find yourself feeling down, disappointed, pessimistic, or de-motivated, then there's a good chance you're sharing mental space with someone who's disengaged. Of course, this is not to say that all disengaged people are miserable in their lives, or that all engaged people are happy.

The disengaged habitually have a self-perception that is markedly different than the way others see them. Maybe Susie claims she hates complaining, yet complain could be her middle name. How about Marie, who alienated her client by talking too much during her presentations, yet perceives herself as quiet and reserved? Maybe you have a relative who thrives on gossip while deprecating another relative for doing the same thing? These are sure signs of people who have failed the self-awareness test and are too disconnected from themselves to have even noticed.

> The wider the gap between our espoused beliefs and our embodied beliefs, the more pain, misery, and suffering we will experience. This gap represents the disconnection between our minds and our hearts, and is the difference between being engaged and not.

We've certainly all been there. While we'd like to think that we're self-reflective and conscious at all times, the fact is that we're not. Not even most of the time. Those of us who have spent decades doing inner work know how easy it is to go on autopilot and provide the same answers to questions that have long since changed. It usually takes a confrontation with a caring and committed friend, or an unfortunate incident, to give us the wake-up call to get us back on our way.

At work, the disengaged person shows up, barely produces enough to get by without being fired, and leaves the moment the bell rings. This person takes advantage of every company benefit, leaves no sick days behind, is the last to volunteer for extra work, and would rather bite off her own arm than give you a hand. She is committed to mediocrity, adequacy, and the status quo. No one is committed to her.

Now let's shift our focus 180 degrees and visit the engaged person. How *do* you know when you've met someone who is fully engaged in her career, in her life, in her relationships? You feel it! Engaged people inspire us without going out of their way to do so. Their presence, the sheer energy of them, ignites something in us that makes us want to be better people. We find their enthusiasm, verve, and vivaciousness infectious. We want what they have even if we can't identify it. There's vibrancy to people who are engaged and the passion within them is electrified with such brilliant wattage that it illuminates everything it touches. They radiate good mojo.

> Engaged people are a flystrip for positive life experiences. They are, in practice, passion magnets that draw love, fun, excitement, and fulfillment to everything they do.

These are the people who most folks are either magically drawn to or inexplicably repelled by. Some people want some of what they have, while others are so intimidated by this undiluted passion that they run screaming from the room.

Engaged people have extraordinary core strength, a relaxed familiarity with themselves, and an immovable sense of identity that enables them to unabashedly, unapologetically live out loud. They often have the courage, the mental stamina, and the requisite emotional resilience to live in the question, "Who am I becoming and what do I want once I achieve that?"

My colleague and friend Dan Diamond is one of these engaged people. You could squeeze the passion out of him like juice from an orange in season. This man bounces into a room with an energy that delights the spirit, invites people to play, and entices them to find the spring in their own step. And that's before he's even said anything. And the guy wears red high-tops—how fun is that!

Dan has a grown-up job: He's a physician. But his God-given job is to celebrate every gosh-darn thing he can get his hands on or his mind around. If you ever meet Dan, ask him about Hurricane Katrina, and make sure you have an extra two hours to listen to some stories. Bring a box of tissues to dry your tears, and also be prepared to get the hiccups from laughing too hard.

I admire this man because he's a walking invitation for the rest of us to get a life and do something personally meaningful with it. I respect him because he makes a contribution wherever he goes. I love him because, like me, he's an exclamation point in a world full of periods.

Engaged people like Dan are easy to spot—regardless of where they fall on the introvert-extrovert continuum, they exude an unmistakable energy that practically screams, "I love my life!" and "I want red high-tops!"

Initiate Impact!

1. In what ways are you engaged with your work and career?
2. How does your level of engagement impact your organization?
3. How does your organization impact your ability to engage?
4. What about it inspires you to joy and fulfillment?
5. If you're not engaged, what's standing in the way of your reconnecting or changing jobs?

Essay 35

"You Are the Rock in Your Own Pond"
Who You Are Impacts Everything You Do

By 5 P.M. today, 1600 women—twice the number of men—will have left corporate America, a travesty given the enormous talent for leadership that women demonstrate. They're leaving because of the glass ceiling; because they're disengaged and disheartened. They're leaving because they don't feel seen, heard, or celebrated. They're leaving for the very same reason that manifests itself as an extra 20 pounds, an unfulfilling relationship, or not enough money. The result of this exodus is untold lost revenue, deteriorating morale, and skyrocketing hiring costs.

These women know that there is more to life than the way they're currently living. They want to bring all of who they are to everything they do; they just don't know how. You know these women: They express their discontent by saying things like, "I'm living someone else's life." "I'm depressed for no reason." "I wish I could trust myself more." "I want to stop talking about what I'm going to do one day, and I just want to go out and *do it*."

Why are American companies hemorrhaging female talent? These women do not know what they want, and therefore have no way of getting "it." Where do you as a manager come in? The degree to which they are disconnected from themselves is a precise measure of their disengagement from your organization. You can count on that. Literally.

The women who are leaving are looking for something—*anything* —to help them reconnect with the parts of themselves they've mislaid (which was likely years before you first met them). And because they are so detached from themselves and isolated from others, most don't even know exactly why they've left, or even what they want. "It" may be expressed as more money, more responsibility, greater flexibility, better visibility, bigger benefits; but "it" is likely something entirely different.

The truth? The "It" they're looking for is identity, validation, and support of Self, with a capital S.

■ ■ ■

Most women have been brainwashed into believing that they must go outside of themselves to improve, change, and become their best selves. They go "out there" to acquire what can only be found "in here." Once we do something better, differently, more, whatever—then we will finally and absolutely become *okay*.

The argument follows, then, that when a woman experiences discontent or dissatisfaction at work, she will go somewhere else and get a better job where people will finally hear, see, celebrate, promote, and recognize her, and pay her fairly. She may blame her plight on her environment because she hasn't done the requisite internal exploration; or she hasn't gone deep enough. She looks outside of herself for reinforcement of her personal power, instead of determining her own destination. It is rare that women stop, reengage themselves at the most basic level, take a spiritual and emotional inventory, and access the truth of that which they seek. Instead, they leave your company, and you pay the price for their exodus. (Perhaps you yourself have had these thoughts, lived this experience, and suffered the consequences of being divorced from yourself?)

So what can you do about it? How do you—and every person who manages female employees—handle this?

> The bottom line implication is that the more fully women are engaged with themselves, the more they will be able to determine what their *it* is, precluding them from unnecessarily leaving your organization.
>
> Note: Engagement results in connection and connection is the key to retention. Period.

Those to whom this applies will want to remember that simple yet profound saying, "Wherever you go, there you are." If you jump ship without fully comprehending why you're doing it, then you'll likely be in the identical place in your new job within a year. You may want to consider that it is highly probable that the source of your discontent may be something emotional and/or spiritual, and actually have nothing to do with your job.

"Who you are has an impact on everything you do." This is the mantra of the quintessentially engaged woman, the inference of which means that every last cell of your spectacular self—your vision, talents, gifts, quirkiness, humor, intelligence—impacts every sector of your life, including, of course, your career. Likewise, any issues that weren't mined—any dark corners, fears, or neuroses—are brought along and unceremoniously displayed for the entire workforce to see.

Do you think that you're different from others? That you do a marvelous job of hiding portions of yourself from your coworkers? That you can actually retrieve those deposited parts of your personality at your office door on your way home? Think again!

■ ■ ■

Let me introduce you to The Solomon Accountability Model™. Visualize that you have thrown a rock into the middle of a pond. Now observe how concentric circles form from the place where the rock met the water. There are probably a dozen or so circles radiating from that epicenter, and each of those circles exists because of the impact that the rock had on the water when it broke its surface. As you stand on the shore, the circle nearest you may be less distinct or defined than

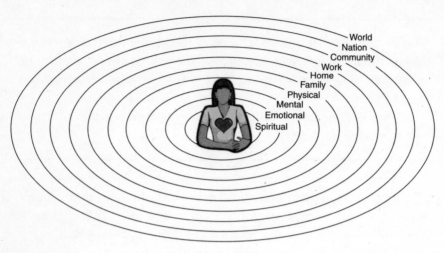

FIGURE 35.1   The Solomon Accountability Model™
ⓒ 2010 Nancy D. Solomon, LLC. All Rights Reserved.

the ones closer to the epicenter; but they are all nonetheless a result of the rock's penetration of the water.

Are you wondering what this has to do with engagement? Everything! We are the rock in our own pond (see Figure 35.1). We, at some level, generate *everything* in our life. Just as that fifth circle out from the center of the pond, for instance, would not have formed had that rock not broken the water's surface; the events in our lives would never have occurred had we—in our infinite though often unconscious wisdom—not instigated them.

Our external world is a three-dimensional expression of who we are at the very core of our existence. Our spiritual, emotional, and mental makeup has repercussions for every other facet of our lives—career, family, health, community, wealth. Nothing in our lives is excluded from this paradigm; there is not a single aspect that doesn't fall into this accountability web.

This theory in and of itself is neither new nor radical. What *is* revolutionary is its induction into the workplace, and the magnitude of what that implies.

While a similar movement two decades ago made the notion of personal responsibility and accountability fairly well known if not well practiced, never before has engagement been a systemic requirement or a basic tenet of business in America. The recent bout of ethics scandals, however, has served to further underscore how the sweeping impact of our values—and lack thereof, leaves no segment of society untainted.

> Our fluid sense of ethics has instigated a global personal crisis.

Wherever I go, I hear about how people are taking a thorough accounting of the intimate side of themselves and becoming critically aware of whom they are. I hear about how this impacts their actions, how they are perceived, and the implication this has on their careers.

There's no dispute that the culture of corporate America is shifting, and that the chasm between who we are and what we do is swiftly closing. Engagement is the measure of the connectedness between those things (see Essay #34). There is an incremental demand for congruency in all areas of our lives, which has resulted in women being increasingly unwilling to leave any portion of themselves behind when they go to work.

Engagement is the interpersonal relationship or commitment between individuals, their work, purpose, and passion. Utilizing our gifts and talents enhances our experiences and expands our capacity to lead. The extent to which we understand *why we do what we do* will result in deeper engagement with the company for which we work.

> When we are on purpose, we have more meaningful and sustainable relationships—first and foremost with ourselves, and secondarily with our coworkers, management, the entire team, and the customer.

We are more gratified, more content, and more passionate than our disheartened counterparts. The net-net is that engaged people are happy people—and happy people stay where they are.

Here's the situation. Women just about everywhere are concerned about this disconnect. They know it. You know it. Businesses know it. Yet many feel ill-equipped to do anything about it, because it is such a daunting undertaking. How do you get women to do the self-awareness work that will help them to understand that they don't feel they deserve to be happy and satisfied—and that this is the very reason they opted out on interviewing for that promotion?

The answer? You can't and you don't. There is nothing you can do to make anyone do personal growth work; nothing. You *can*, however, step up your efforts to invite these women to bring all of themselves to work; and you can do this by creating a work environment that is conducive to encouraging women to:

- Speak their truth
- Take healthy risks
- Be controversial when appropriate
- Be innovative
- Ask for what they want
- Be strategic in their career planning
- Support other women
- Have work/life balance
- Value their contributions
- Acknowledge themselves
- Get appropriate recognition
- Express their ambition
- Lead in their own style

What will this accomplish? Well, for one thing, it will make you feel great about yourself and your leadership abilities. Secondly, it will empower these women to empower themselves by raising their self-esteem. As a manager, you have a much greater chance of successfully inspiring a woman to explore her inner sanctum if she's feeling positive about herself. She'll be a lot more interested in searching for her life purpose if she already feels like a respected and worthwhile contributor.

While some businesses have taken giant leaps into the personal and, therefore, professional development of their employees, many others have merely tiptoed around the subject. The yardstick, as always, is people. When you create an open, honest, transparent culture rich in integrity, you will have a population of people eager to be the rocks in their own pond. They will be excited about the opportunities that accountability presents, and they'll have enough skin in the game to invest the time and attention necessary to get their personal needs met.

Initiate Impact!

1. Have you ever had a job where you felt obligated to leave part of who you are at the door?
   - How did that feel? How did it impact your job performance?
2. What emotional/spiritual qualities do you have that are most critical to your job satisfaction?
   - How do these impact your job performance?
3. Make a list of the times in your life when your personal issues either positively or negatively impacted your career.
   - What did you learn?
4. Make a list of the times in your life when career issues either positively or negatively impacted your personal life.
   - What did you learn?

Essay 36

A Woman's Heart and Spirit
Courage at Work

Shellie was in the training program of a major Realtor in the northeast. Her group worked exceedingly long hours and every night they'd leave the office, en masse, and go for dinner and drinks at the local pub. One night the regional VP, a man twice Shellie's age, hit on her. She knew if she resisted him the new promotion she was promised would vaporize. So she didn't. Thirty years later, she still carries that shame.

Margaret's boss was belligerent, crude, and a walking sexist joke. Margaret found him and his behavior intolerable. Rather than say anything to him, she quit before she found another job.

Leonia discovered, while putting together the largest proposal of her career, that the numbers she'd been given from accounting were incorrect: By over $4 million. First she freaked out. Then she screamed at accounting. Finally she asked for a transfer, relieving herself from ever having to confront the prospective client.

> *"Courage is not the absence of fear. Courage is the strength to act wisely when we are most afraid."*
> —Mary Fisher, artist, author, and AIDS activist

It takes a lot of courage to stand up to our challengers. It is not that Shellie, Margaret, and Leonia weren't courageous—indeed they were. Their stories all occurred over 30 years ago, well before we had the choices we do now. What made them courageous? They stayed in the workforce, each handling her situation with as much dignity as she could. Courage, in this context, means staying in the game and writing your own rules. It means following your gut over someone else's guidance. It means stating your truth even if no one else shares that with you. It means showing up—authentically, accountably, and unapologetically.

This is everyday courage, the kind of courage in which fear is always calibrated, is always a consideration. It is the courage it takes to be a woman. To be a workingwoman. To be a workingwoman with children. To be a single workingwoman with children. It is the courage it takes to be *you*.

What is baffling is that virtually every dictionary definition of the word courage explicitly states that courage means to face difficulty, conflict, pain, and battle *without fear*. Are these people for real?

We're not talking about Extreme Courage CSI, we're talking about life—namely yours. Fear is a variable in every human condition. End of story. It is a part of life, not an exception to it. If you never feel fear you're either over-medicated or in denial. Either way, you may want to consider professional help.

Courage has a high degree of relevancy for women in the business world. The courage we must summon, the courage we must dig deep for is to face those challenges common to all women: to take an unpopular stand, and to take professional risks that, more than likely, we have never been prepared for. Twenty-first century courage requires us to go inward to our heart, spirit, and intuition for guidance, and to stem the intrusion of external input.

The word *courage* is derived from the French word, *corage*, which means heart and spirit. The male concept of courage, as I'm learning from my seven-year-old son, Benjamin, involves something detonating, crashing, blazing or otherwise creating loud and obnoxious noises, to say nothing of the fumes. Given that "male" is our cultural standard, little attention is paid to the feminine portrayal of courage, which, in part, accounts for why we deny it or push back when someone assigns us that label (see Essay #28). We do not go into battle, we do not blow things up (okay, maybe we do that with issues, but that's another essay), and we would never consider identifying ourselves as fearless (nor do we strive to be).

We endeavor to live from the inside out, following our hearts and souls where they take us (with the help of our minds and bodies), while avoiding words usually applied to us when we manage to actually do that—words similar to those that can be found in Essay #15 on shrinking to fit. When we stand up for ourselves, when we refuse to budge and thereby take the chance of being called difficult, when we are not swayed by the undertow of politics, we earn the crown of *too*. Too aggressive, too bitchy, too ambitious, too loud—too. Being courageous does not insinuate that this crown doesn't bother us. It's just that we have enough courage to act as though it doesn't.

Initiate Impact!

1. How do you define courage for yourself?
2. What is the most courageous thing you have ever done?
   - Why did you do it?
   - What did you learn about yourself?
   - How will you apply this learning to your career?
3. How does the company you work for, or the one you own, impact your ability to act courageously?
4. What did you learn from your family of origin that
   - Supports courageous acts?
   - Precludes courageous acts?

Essay 37

Move toward Innovative Thinking
Risky Business

Although it may seem to be counterintuitive to those stepping up the leadership ladder, you should realize that your manager wants you to take more risks. That's right—*more* risks. In the past 18 years, I've yet to meet a single senior executive who's said, "Gee, I wish my talent would play it safe and keep things status quo."

But what kind of risk do I mean? And why would your boss encourage his or her employees to take more of them? After all, the word "risk" usually implies exposure to danger, and the possibility that something unwelcome or unsafe is imminent.

> The concerns about risk in corporate America revolve around managers wanting their talent not so much to step *away* from safe decisions; but to move *toward* innovative thinking.

These leaders are cultivating their talent's willingness to drill down deep within themselves to access the confidence that it takes to think differently: This next generation of leaders must trust themselves enough to take risks. Since these managers are successful people themselves, it's likely they hired you *because* of your unique skill set and they want you to use it.

The willingness to take risks is particularly critical during tough economic times. There is a cultural tendency to want to play it safe when times are uncertain. However, if we examine historical precedent, we'll find that it was those who threw the dice in an exciting and new direction who were most triumphant at making the changes that the times demanded.

What makes employees reluctant to take risks at work? In a word: *FEAR*.

They are often afraid that:

- I'm not smart enough.
- I'm not educated enough.
- I'll look stupid.
- I'll be wrong.
- I can't trust my gut instincts.
- I won't get the sale anyway.
- Things will change. I hate change.
- _____
- _____

These things don't have to be real; they just have to be perceived that way. To be sure, there is nothing that will prevent or halt forward movement (and therefore, risk-taking behavior) quicker than the prospect of your ego getting bruised or annihilated in the process.

What does a great manager want you to do?

- Have confidence in who you are and what you do.
- Trust yourself.
- Follow your gut instincts.
- Don't rely on "It's always been done that way."
- Be willing to be wrong.
- Think uniquely.
- Take the initiative.

The next time you're facing a situation that requires you to step out of your safety zone, ask yourself these questions:

1. ***Is the risk perceived or real?*** Do the facts or evidence over-whelmingly stack against your position, or are you simply afraid of the unknown?
2. ***Are you taking this risk to prove who you are (your ego) or to demonstrate it (your heart)?*** Are you taking a bold stand because you know in your bones that this is the right course; or are you trying to prove that you're smart and competent?
3. ***Is the timing right?*** Your idea might be simply brilliant at some point; just not now.
4. ***What is the best possible outcome of taking this risk?*** In an ideal world, what's the outcome? What are the wins?
5. ***What's the worst possible outcome?*** Think disaster. Do you have a backup plan? Will anything be beyond repair?
6. ***If you didn't succeed, how would you recover?*** This is called Plan B. Have you fully prepared a plan for the possibility that you might not be able to go back to the way things were before you took this risk?
7. ***If you failed, what might you be able to learn?*** You've not met your goals before. It will happen again. What wisdom have you gleaned from this event? If you got a do-over, what, if anything, would you do differently?

So what's the risk of *not* taking risks? When you don't take risks, things stay the same; and same is *not* necessarily why you were recruited. *Same* may mean no new opportunities, little growth, that the project never gets launched, that you're passed over for that promotion, and that you end up feeling underutilized or devalued. Change one letter—and *same* and *safe* are spelled, well, the same. Curious, huh?

Initiate Impact!

1. What's one risk you could take in your job, right now, that would positively impact your organization or your own business?
2. What is the potential downside of this risk?
3. What is the potential upside?
4. Who can champion this risk with you?

Essay 38

Did She Jump or Was She Pushed?

Retaining Top Female Talent

Me: Did you tell HR the real reason why you left?

Her: Well, no, not exactly.

Me: Why not?

Her: I didn't want my HR manager to feel bad. I didn't want her to think it was her fault.

Me: So, you didn't want to hurt her feelings?

Her: No. Well, maybe. Sorta. Yeah, I guess I didn't want to hurt her feelings.

Me: And you wanted her to like you?

Her: When you say it like that, it sounds awful. Okay, so I wanted HR to like me; to approve of me even though I'd resigned. Besides, I didn't want to burn any bridges.

Me: Is there anything else, any other reason you held back?

Her: What difference would it have made if I told HR truthfully why I was leaving? I'd already made up my mind to go. The damage had already been done. And if my manager ever found out how I really felt about her—

Me: So, in essence, you lied to her because you wanted to look good, you wanted the company to look favorably on you, and you felt powerless to impact the company you'd help build?

Her: Pretty much.

240

Me: Tell me something. How will the company ever "get it"; how will they change a broken system if people like you don't tell them the truth? How will they ever see that employee dissatisfaction and poor morale isn't an anomaly, but a fact of life in your company?

Her: Well, if they don't get it already, what am I supposed to do? They'll think it's only me, that I'm just a complainer. Besides, I never feel like they hear me anyway.

■ ■ ■

This was a verbatim conversation.

I have had some variation of this identical dialogue with 26 other women over the past 12 months. The only factors that varied were the amount of anger and frustration the women experienced; the length of time it took them to decide to "retire"; and the degree to which the woman felt impotent to impact her organization.

> When a woman says, "What difference would it make?" what she means is, "What difference do *I* make?"

Because she felt invisible in her job, which is one of the reasons she's leaving, she feels invisible when she resigns as well. Because she didn't know the difference she made in her job, she thinks it won't make any difference to you that she's leaving it.

An avalanche of research has unequivocally concluded that women are leaving their jobs and careers for reasons that are personal, political, and, most often, both. We're told that we're leaving because of the glass ceiling, because we're disengaged, and because we don't feel seen, heard, or celebrated (those are my words). Although this information has been determined by research, surveys, and exit interviews, my question is: Is it the truth? Or is this a convenient explanation that has deteriorated into an oversimplified excuse?

Tell us: Why are you leaving? Where are you going? Did you "jump"? Did you wake up one day and say to yourself, "That's it! Stick a fork in me, I'm done"?

Were you "pushed?" Were you left before you'd made plans to leave? Did you stay where you were, and complain about it for another year or two, suffering from a severe case of "presenteeism" (see Essay #18), where your body showed up at work but your enthusiasm, energy, and psyche stayed home?

Go ahead, check which ones could apply to you.

☐ I want more flexibility.
☐ I am tired of banging my head up against the glass ceiling.
☐ I want/need/deserve more money.
☐ I feel invisible.
☐ My contributions aren't recognized or valued.
☐ I am tired of being passed over for promotions.
☐ I don't feel heard.
☐ I'm not taken seriously.
☐ I want more freedom.
☐ I want more opportunities.
☐ _____
☐ _____

What is most disturbing is not so much that we're leaving the corporate world: It's why we're leaving—and the impact that these reasons have on our lives and the organizations that employ us—that is most perturbing. Irrespective of the public version of the story called "I'm departing to start my own business or to become a full-time mom," I have long suspected that women all over the country, from entry level to upper level manager, frequently provide justifications for leaving corporate America that are, in reality, lies of commission or omission. Armed with politically correct jargon—and the proclivity to seek approval and preserve relationships—we will craft a departure statement that is only distantly related to the truth. It stands to reason that our impetus for exiting is likely the same reason we felt we couldn't honestly answer the question, "Why are you leaving?" to begin with.

Consider this: One of the many reasons we're hitting the glass ceiling is that we repeatedly start over in new jobs; when the going gets tough, we leave. Every time we have a do-over we forfeit our tenure. Were we to stay put, forthrightly addressing our concerns, then we would accrue the seniority needed to implement the changes we seek.

Women have been socialized to be the custodian of our relationships before our own feelings. Divulging our secrets to HR might have made our manager feel inadequate, incompetent, or responsible. Heaven forbid! Fabricating a story seems a more palatable option to most of us. Put yourself in your manager's shoes—wouldn't you want people to be candid with you so you could effectively do your job?

> The inability to stem the outward flow of women causes many managers to look no further than absolutely necessary at the motivation of those migrating from their ranks.

It is de rigueur to place fault on us for being "not enough" of something or "too much" of something else. It is reasoned that we leave our jobs simply because we couldn't "make it." Well, maybe we didn't want to make it or we got tired of trying—or simply don't know how.

Baffled by this mass desertion, the system, the women, the management, and the culture are all blamed—all of which only serves to perpetuate the dynamics that were the initial catalyst for her departure. Now add to this mix the fact that there are women who are bailing without truly knowing why; and you have one, messy, self-sustaining situation: These rare few know that something isn't working for them, but they are unable or unwilling to figure out what it is. So they leave. (More on that in Essay #35.)

What deserves to be acknowledged, if not celebrated, is that it may not have been a case of opting out, but rather an act of personal power for these women to say, "Company XYZ doesn't understand what I need."

> "I've had enough of going to the hardware store and being disappointed that I don't find any bread. I'm going to find myself a bakery."

I coach and consult with many of these women. I have the privilege of being one of the few to whom they confide while they're making the excruciatingly difficult decision to leave their well-earned careers—or after that decision's been made for them. What do they tell me? Listen in for a moment:

- I want to bring all of myself to work!
- I hate that I have to pretend that I'm not a woman who has to act like a guy in order to get ahead—which is exactly what I have to do.
- I'm tired of having to leave pieces of myself at home in order to survive here.
- This place exhausts me—I don't feel like I'm welcomed.
- They make it too hard for women to work here.
- If I want to get promoted, I know exactly who I need to be—and that is *not* who I am!
- _____
- _____

Beneath the story line, beyond the politics, aside from the corporate-speak lies a woman's primal need to rebirth who she was before she forgot; and to recall her answer to the question: "What do you want?"

■ ■ ■

> In truth, she does not leave you; She does not leave her career. In truth, her exodus from corporate America is, in effect, a journey back to her core Self.

I wonder, and I invite you to do the same, what changes need to be made and how fast we can make them, so that these women can find their core selves right where they are, in your small business. or in corporate America. Imagine the power of helping her in that quest, and the impact that would have on all the resulting relationships!

There is a giant AND in the corporate exodus conversation that trails off into oblivion, because it is just too big and too cumbersome for most organizations to tackle. Yes, these women are leaving for logical, practical, rational reasons; *and* there is an indelible dotted line between their withdrawal and the spiritual and emotional crisis in our country today.

There's a trend that's worth mentioning here. The good news is that it only applies to a small number of women; the bad news is that it gives the *appearance* of applying to most women. That said, there are many women who notoriously, unfortunately, and for currently unidentified reasons have little empathy, compassion, or tolerance for their sisters who opt out. A lot of these female execs make no attempt to stand at the exit door, thwarting these women's escape. Nor are they giving them a congratulatory slap on the back with "Way to go, girlfriend!" either. We have come to expect that a disproportionate number of women will prematurely leave their careers; and managers have become both resigned to, and hardened by, that fact. We may want to percolate on that!

> When you drill down into it, beneath all the rhetoric and the politics, the root of the problem of *mass desertion* is pure and simple: it's a *relationship* issue!

Yes, that again.

She Jumped
1. Not asking for what she wants
2. Invisibility: both agreed to and initiated
3. Shortage of highly visible female role models

4. Networking laterally to the exclusion of networking up
5. Diminished self-awareness/self-engagement
6. Conflict avoidance
7. Not strategically approaching career
8. Lack of mentors
9. Feeling of exclusion
10. _____
11. _____

She Was Pushed
1. Not adequately addressing employee's concerns
2. Risk-avoidant environment
3. Conflict-avoidant environment
4. Short-sightedness
5. Outside recruitment to the exclusion of internal promotion
6. Lack of availability of manager
7. Inadequate communication
8. Inadequate flexible work arrangements
9. Unrealistic workloads
10. Resistance to honest feedback
11. Not encouraging work / life balance
12. _____
13. _____

It's a two-sided equation, to be sure, and not a balanced one; but an equation, nonetheless. Yes, it is imperative that your organization implements every available tactic to attract, train, and retain talent. What needs to be at the top of that list? Training women to lead!

- How they can determine what they want
- How they can become the strategic architects of their careers
- How to get what it is they say they want
- How to hold them accountable for their own learning and leadership? (See Essay #35.)

Filling in these glaring gaps in women's learning, both personally and professionally, will greatly enhance their impact on your organization.

Leaders aren't born, they're grown.

Now, for the other side of that equation: I don't know about you, but I've had enough of hearing about the big bad companies and what they *didn't* do for their employees. Relationships are made up of two or more people; one party is never entirely at fault. Yes, it is your moral and business imperative to make sure that your organization's female employees have every (equal) opportunity to lead and succeed. *And* it is up to the woman, herself, to maximize every one of those opportunities; to be in charge of her destiny. Ultimately, women are accountable for their lives, careers, learning, and leadership skills. Women must become more solution-oriented and less problem-focused. They must to be taught how to cultivate their personal power, to discover their life purpose and to use their gifts and talents: *The main ingredients for them to have impact and for you to retain them.*

Initiate Impact!

1. If you worked in the perfect organization, what would it look like?
  ◆ What would your job description be?
  ◆ How would it feel?
  ◆ Get as many details down as possible.
2. With that done, what is standing in your way of having that job?
3. As a manager how do you impact your staff?
4. As a manager, how does your organization impact your staff?

Essay 39

The Last Taboo
Spirituality at Work

In the early 1980s I worked at Saks Fifth Avenue in the dress department. My buyer went overseas on business during a regularly scheduled management meeting and I was invited to sit in for her. Mr. G, the merchandise manager, had set the agenda to discuss various ways to increase sales. I was a brand spanking new, wet behind the ears, assistant buyer and I saw this as the perfect opportunity to show everyone how clever I was. Seriously.

The buyers went around the table providing suggestions and, when it was my turn, I was so excited with what I was going to share, that I stood up to talk—not the brightest idea considering Mr. G was standing next to me. We were the same height when I was sitting and he was standing. In high heels I was about 6′3″. Mr. G, in heels, was 5′2″. Are you getting the picture? Anyway, back to my clever idea.

Me: Shopping should be fun, right? And the more fun we have, the less likely it is that we'll care about spending too much. So, what I think we need to do is focus on our relationship with our customers—start doing some really nice things like writing them notes thanking them for their business, and keeping track of what they buy. This way we can let them know when something special comes in, and it's a terrific way for our salespeople to develop a real relationship with our customers. Because I think

248

that the better the relationship we have with our customers, the more likely they'll come to Saks and not to our competition. Waddya think?

Mr. G: Thank you for sharing, Nancy. You can sit down now.

I was dismissed. Just like that! From the snickers around the table and the look of annoyance on his face as he strained to look up at me, I knew that this had not gone as well as I'd planned. I sat down.

■ ■ ■

Of course the ideas I brought up in that meeting are now standard practice—we even have a name for it: Relationship Marketing or Good Business Sense. But back in the 1980s it was, to say the least, unorthodox to cross the invisible line between the salesperson and the customer.

Boundaries were unambiguous back then: Our lives were compartmentalized into two distinct categories, personal and business. The expectation was that when we arrived at work, our personal lives were left at the door. No discussion about it. There would be no mention of politics, religion, sex, family, none of it, for that eight to twelve hours a day. To do so was considered "unprofessional."

Fast forward 25 years and we've made more than a little progress in practically and powerfully integrating relationships into everything we do. Whether it's our relationship with our manager, our customer, or our spouse, we know that it's vital to both our personal and professional success; and, of course, the most important relationship we have is with ourselves.

Now, in the twenty-first century, when corporate America has only recently become comfortable embracing the warm fuzzys of relationships, we have a brand new frontier, Spirituality—The Last Taboo.

Uncensored discourse on diversity, gay marriage, ethnicity, stem cell research, you name it, has conveniently paved the way for God to come to work. Hallelujah!

It is interesting, yet not entirely unpredictable, that God is juxta-posed with our increasingly lenient values and decaying ethics. We are an adolescent nation, developmentally speaking. And while on one end of the seesaw we have the self-indulgent behavior of a teenager, we are managing to balance it on the other end with a higher power, steeped in sacred (and patriarchal) traditions. An adolescent expresses his or her independence, tests limits and boundaries, and, upon completion of said experiments, retreats to the safety, stability, and familiarity of the family. Similarly, on one side we have our country pushing the en-velope to destinations unknown to us just a short time ago; and we're maintaining our equilibrium, by seeking comfort in the sanctity of our spiritual beliefs on the other side.

Like me, have you ever wondered why we ever tricked ourselves into believing that our hearts were discordant with corporate culture—when it's actually what makes the culture beat?

Every time I hear someone refer to a corporation making a decision, it makes me want to jump up like a jack-in-the-box and scream like a lunatic. *People* made those corporate decisions: emotional people with families, friends, problems, bills, and rising health costs. A corporation exists only on paper.

Think, for a moment, about "business as usual"—any number of people sitting next to one another day in and day out supposedly having left their heart and soul at home. Puts the "dis" in dysfunction, doesn't it?

Patriarchy is in the process of transitioning to a more holistic model: A heart-centered, more compassionate framework is replacing the outside-in leadership model where we sought our self-esteem from what we did in the material world rather than who we are in the spiritual/emotional one. This is a whole different slant on reorganiza-tion, isn't it?

Women are anything but reluctant spiritual warriors: Some of you have been trained to "act like a man" and to park your personality next to your car in the company lot. You seek a higher power anyway—you'll take autonomy anywhere you can find it, anywhere you can create it. Some of you have been raised with strong, powerful, charismatic role models who fought the fight for your generation; but some of you don't even know what fight we boomer babes are talking about. You act entitled and we resent that, while also admiring you for having so internalized your power that you have no need to discuss it. While we want a large dollop of the self-esteem you were born with, we don't want to give up telling our war stories. I'm not sure if this is a good thing or not.

None of this is going to change as much as it needs to until the spiritual and emotional doors are swung completely open. We're learning how to be women *and* be leaders *and* be present. We don't need one more thing on our perpetual to-do list. A "to be" list would be most appreciated, however. Just imagine it:

☐ Pick up dry cleaning   DO

☐ 10 minutes speaking with inner wisdom   BE

☐ Bring children to school   DO

☐ 5 minutes of self-acknowledgement time   BE

☐ Pay bills   DO

☐ 10 minutes writing gratitude list   BE

☐ Respond to work emails   DO

☐ _____

☐ _____

We want to bring to light our authentic self and grow to be comfortable with, and in appreciation of, the woman we discover we are destined to be. We're ardent in our mission to reveal our life purpose, to use our gifts and talents, and to make public our passion. When that is accomplished, we will have more energy, more time, more enthusiasm and more creativity to bring to work.

Disconnection from our spiritual center is tantamount to having a car with no engine, or a computer without a hard drive. A woman's spirituality is her anchor, the very marrow of her bones. Perhaps that's why so many employees jump at the chance to participate in Volunteer Day or Give Back Day. It's finally an opportunity to engage a part of themselves that's usually absent from work. Ideology like "personally meaningful difference" is becoming the most resource-rich currency of the generations entering the workforce.

Almost every day I speak to a woman who tells me she's spiritually inquisitive, depleted, or questing. If your business doesn't at least acknowledge this hunger, or even feed it, someone else's will. People who are ready to move forward will do just about anything to reengage with their core self. The more technology saturated they become, the more complicated their lives, the more they are crammed with "stuff" and information and to-dos, the more they will feel the internal pressure, the calling within them to return to the organic comfort of the heart (where, by the bye, their spirit lives).

Past the emotional remnants of our families of origin, beyond the stereotypes and the expectations of our ethnicity, beneath the fear that self-disclosing genuineness will lead to the annihilation of society, there is a soft, insistent voice that's been whispering to us since we can remember. By design, I don't know what your inner voice says, but mine perpetually reminds me to "Be still. Let go. Relax. Trust yourself." And yours? _____

_____

_____
_____

_____

Women are (finally) acknowledging, out loud, that this is not the voice of their imagination—that this voice is solid, dependable, and eternal. This is the voice of your inner wisdom, your Soul, your intuition, your spirit, God. This is a voice that has always been with you, will never leave you, won't downsize you, and won't ever lay you off. It will never make you redundant or insignificant, it will never outsource itself, and it will never wait a year to give you a promotion. This is the voice of Truth—your truth—and it is in that expanse that invincible women stand.

> Women hear their inner voices; they just haven't
> always trusted them.

Who is the woman who is reading this book? Who is looking to give herself permission to be at one with the spirit within her? She is the woman sitting next to you at a client meeting. She is your friend, your chairman of the board, your admin, your mother, and the president of your bank. She is you.

Just about 20 years ago, when I first started my public speaking career, I began the ritual of taking the spiritual temperature of my audience by asking: "Raise your hand if you would call yourself spiritual, and you define spiritual for yourself." In a crowd of 50, one or two brave souls might timidly raise their hands about head high and immediately retreat to more popular ground. Fifteen years ago, maybe 10 percent of the audience would publicly "own" their relationship with their personal brand of God. Ten years ago half the audience, regardless of size, would fess up. And five years ago, maybe three-quarters would. I recently spoke to 3,000 women at a direct sales company, more than half of them Gen X and Gen Yers. From the stage, I counted fewer than a dozen hands *not* raised.

> *"Spirituality at work is past its tipping point, and on
> the verge of becoming a trend."*
> —Nancy D. Solomon

I have spent countless hours contemplating what's changed and why. Are people becoming more spiritual? Are we just willing to talk about it more? And either way, why?

I admit that I still tread carefully when I raise the subject of God, more in business circumstances than in social ones. Our relationship with the divine is the most intimate relationship we will ever have. The word *God* acts as a hair-trigger. Once God is brought into a conversation, it takes about three seconds for people to bring to mind everything they have wrapped around that relationship; every positive and negative trigger gets fired. Once it's introduced, the conversation at once becomes both more intimate and political.

My ambition is not to cast a vote on anyone's experience with God in any direction. My intention is always to invite people to bring the relationship they have with God into the relationship I am having with them. The speech bubble over my head reads: "It's okay to talk about your spirituality here. I know that you are a spiritual being and this, too, is a part of you that I'm curious and excited about."

For many it is merely a relief, a sign of trust that we no longer have to guard this "secret" that God guides our life. Rare is the person who stands still in the conversation about God, especially in an environment not generally associated with spirituality. People either edge forward or push back. Hard. The person who seemingly edges forward almost visibly bonds with me, even if we haven't gotten to the part of the conversation where his or her beliefs are revealed. Just the mere mention, the "permission" to talk about it, deepens the connection we have. Not because I share their beliefs but because we have the space in our relationship to have differences, to bring up taboos, and to be ourselves.

Are you concerned that if you tolerate, allow, or invite your employees to bring their spirituality to work that you'll create unwelcome religious fervor? That things will get out of control? That people will commit holy wars? Put all of that down. The objective is to deliberately create an environment of mutual respect that would discourage proselytizing and misbehaving, in general.

Here's the deal: People who believe in a higher power, or who follow a religion, or who believe in God are bringing this with them to work whether or not you extend permission for them to do so. All you are doing is creating an environment in which they now feel comfortable doing what they've been doing all along. In other words, you don't have to do anything; you just need to stay out of the way.

Yes, the more you make room at the table for diversity, the greater the chance that things can get messy *and* the greater the chance that the conversation will be lively, innovative, creative, and productive. Most companies have some form of dress code. Most companies have some form of ethics code. Do you see any reason that you couldn't collaborate with your team to come up with a faith-friendly code? Just as you do for other high impact issues, trust your team; trust that they can self-monitor, make excellent choices, and have enough skin in the game to make a personally meaningful difference. Isn't that why you hired them?

Initiate Impact!

1. What role, if any, does your spirituality play in your life?

2. How does your spirituality impact your professional endeavors?

3. How does the company you work for, or the company you own, impact your spirituality?

4. In an ideal world, what faith-friendly code would you like to see in your organization?

5. What, if anything, is standing in the way of your initiating a faith-friendly code?

Afterword

"It is who we become as a result of the experience, not the experience itself, which is most valuable."

—Nancy D. Solomon

It's a good thing that we don't know what we don't know or we might never do anything that requires vast amounts of courage, like having children or writing a book.

Both are regarded as noble as well as necessary; both are choices; both leave stretch marks on our heart.

Impact! is exactly as I'd first envisioned it five years ago. The content is the same, as is its objective. The format was modified—only the title dramatically changed. I, on the other hand, had already outgrown my experience of myself by the time I completed the introduction. True to the message of this book, I know precisely what I came here to do, although it took me five years to get out of my own way and get it done. Regularly I doubted myself and my vision, which prompted me to go outside of myself and collaborate with masses of people who knew me, as well as virtual strangers who didn't, all in an effort to validate what I already knew. Have you ever done that?

In the end, I left more out of this book than I had room to put in, I became ever more the student than the teacher, and I had far more questions than answers. In the end, I remembered who I am. Which, of course, is the point of this book: to remember who you are and what you came to do, so you can be sure to get it done. So that you can have impact!

My hope for you, the reader, is that this journey we've taken together has been most valuable to you; that it has opened doors both familiar and new; that it has resolved old questions while birthing new ones; that it has challenged the places you've grown too comfortable and comforted the places you've long felt challenged. My desire for you is that you remember who *you* are.

If I had magic fairy dust I would have loved to personally shared your evolution with you, to have witnessed the places where you grew and stretched and transformed beyond your own limitations and expectations. I would have cherished counting the number of times the light bulbs went off above your head when you recognized your self-worth, and owned how lovable you truly are. It would have been grand fun to have swiped at the tears of self-awareness when you discovered that you were perfect all along. It would have been my privilege to help you throw your old beliefs against a wall like china on brick, and to assist you to sweep up afterward.

Whatever you accomplished, I celebrate you. You do the same. My parting invitation is for you to know that *"where you are is a cause for celebration, not an apology."*

I'm not very good at goodbyes, so rather than look at the end of this book as the end of our relationship, I'd rather consider it the beginning—much like your relationship with yourself, as of today. With that outcome in mind, I've created the website, www.from invisibletoinvincible.com, to support you to become more of who you were meant to be. Come visit me there, download the assessments, play with the exercises, become part of our community, enjoy the articles, and post *your* story—your journey from invisible to invincible. I look forward to hearing from you! Write me at nancy@frominvisibletoinvincible.com.

Be seen. Be heard. Be celebrated. Be yourself.

With much love and gratitude,

Nancy

Winter 2009

Bibliography

The Allianz Women Money & Power Study. August 2006. https://www.allianzlife .com/WomenMoneyPower/Default.aspx

Babcock, Linda and Sara Laschever *Women Don't Ask: Negotiation and the Gender Divide*. Princeton: Princeton University Press, 2003.

Business Women's Network. 2005 WOW! Quick Facts: Women and Diversity. Washington, D.C.: Diversity Best Practices (DBP), 2005.

Catalyst Organization. *The Double-Bind Dilemma for Women in Leadership: Damned if You Do, Doomed if You Don't*. The Catalyst Organization, 2007 (July).

Coffman, Curt, and Gabriel Gonzalez-Molina. *Follow This Path: How the World's Greatest Organizations Drive Growth by Unleashing Human Potential*. New York: Warner Books, 2002.

Fels, Anna. "Do Women Lack Ambition?" *Harvard Business Review* (April 2004).

Greenberg, P. E., R. C. Kessler, H. G. Birnbaum, S. A. Leong, S. W. Lowe, P. A. Berglund, and P. K. Corey-Lisle. "The Economic Burden of Depression in the United States: How Did It Change between 1990 and 2000? *Journal of Clinical Psychiatry* 64: 12 (December 2003):1465–75.

The Harris Poll #11. February 26, 2003 http://www.harrisinteractive.com/harris_ poll/index.asp?pid=359

Loehr, Jim and Tony Schwartz. *The Power of Full Engagement: Managing Energy, Not Time Is the Key to Full Engagement and Optimal Performance*. New York: The Free Press, 2003.

Morris, Jon D., Chongmoo Woo, James A. Geason, and Joojoung Kim. "The Power of Affect: Predicting Intention." *Journal of Advertising Research* (2002): 1–14.

Widmeyer Research & Polling. Poll commissioned by the Center for a New American Dream. Washington, DC: August 2003.

The Harris Poll #11. February 26, 2003 http://www.harrisinteractive.com/harris_ poll/index.asp?pid=359

August 9, 2007 http://www.adherents.com/Religions_By_Adherents.html

YouTube.com. 15 June 2007. http://www.youtube.com/watch?v=WjlsVHY-CXM

Index

About the Author

As a writer, speaker, facilitator, and executive coach, Nancy D. Solomon has built her career around one simple question: *"What did you come here to do, and are you getting it done?"*

Over the last 18 years, Nancy has inspired thousands to remove the barriers to fulfilling their life's purpose. Whether focusing on company-wide results or individual success, she starts with one essential point of engagement—people's connection with themselves.

As her work with both organizations and individuals has repeatedly shown, bottom line results come from taking a holistic approach to people: one that incorporates the physical, mental, emotional, and spiritual.

In her first career incarnation, Nancy was a special education teacher, but, disillusioned by the politics of education, she switched to the fashion industry, working for such corporate giants as Saks Fifth Avenue and Calvin Klein. While she was very well-paid, Nancy felt unfulfilled.

As Vice President of Sales for North America for a European corporation, she asked herself, *"How much money will it take for me to forget how much I hate my life?"* The question inspired her to finally pursue her true passion—helping people to *"turn their potential into performance."*

With a master's degree in psychology and 18 years coaching experience, Nancy travels the country evangelically spreading the word that *"You get in life what you have the courage to ask for."* She has inspired thousands to remove the obstacles to personal and professional success and to engage in their work and in their lives. That may be why she's been called a cross between Dr. Phil in a skirt and "Conversations with God."

President and founder of WomenThink.com and TheSolomon Solutions.com, Nancy counts among her clients Microsoft, Nordstrom, Target, Acura, Sheraton, dozens of small businesses, and many potentially passionate individuals and organizations.

She can be contacted at nancy@frominvisibletoinvincible.com.